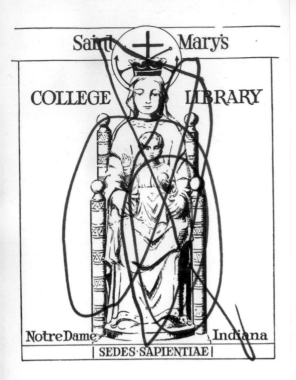

Cities of the World:

BRUSSELS

Cities of the World:

BRUSSELS

K. M. WILLCOX

SOUTH BRUNSWICK
NEW YORK: A. S. BARNES AND CO., INC.

Library of Congress Catalogue Card Number:66-24928

A. S. Barnes and Co., Inc.

South Brunswick, New Jersey

6513
Printed in the United States of America

Contents

List of Illustrations

Author's Note

MY SINCERE thanks are due to 'Inbel'—the Belgian Ministry of Information, for making this book possible.

Its director, M. Ugeux, and M. d'Arian of his staff, made all the plans, and the latter, with Mme d'Arian and their delightful schoolgirl daughter, Anne (who can most capably do this kind of thing by herself), helped me to carry them out.

In addition, I would thank Mlle van Haelewyck, Press Attaché at the Belgian Embassy in London, and all others who have so kindly entertained me and provided me with information from time to time.

June 1965.   K. M. W.

Chapter 1

'Cité en Forme de Cœur'

CITY in the form of a heart. So its own people name Brussels. The city in the form of a heart is most clearly to be seen on any street map of Brussels. For the ancient riverside settlement of Broecksele had a rampart round it for defensive purposes and the line which that followed was exactly heart-shaped. Later, when the town outgrew the tight confines of the surrounding wall and another was built beyond it, the old rampart was pulled down and its place taken by a ring road, which still plainly shows the heart-shaped outline.

Belgium is a land of two languages, French and Flemish, and a line separating it into a northern half, where Flemish predominates, and a southern, where French is spoken, passes quite near to Brussels. The city is almost equidistant from all the country's frontiers, including the one which is the sea, so that it would seem to have been predestined to become the capital.

But it bids fair to be more than this. Already it is the seat of Benelux, that customs union of Belgium, the Netherlands and Luxembourg, of the European Common Market and of a number of other international organizations. Much of this is again the result of the city's position, for to look at a map of western Europe is to see at a glance how fittingly Brussels is placed to become a focal point of western European movement and life. It is possible to think of it as the centre of two or three concentric rings of cities, all names on any one ring being roughly at the same distance from it. Thus Amsterdam, Düsseldorf, Cologne, Luxembourg and Calais are all less than two hundred kilometres away; a group including London, Paris, Hamburg and Frankfort lies within the five-hundred-kilometre range, while there are a great number of important cities round the eleven- and twelve-hundred mark: Oslo, Stockholm, Warsaw, Budapest, Rome and Barcelona are among these.

Furthermore, the great transatlantic flow of traffic between west and east in either direction, whether moving by sea or by air, finds for itself convenient arrival and departure points none of which is at any great distance from Brussels: London Airport, Orly (Paris), Schiepol (Amsterdam), and the seaports of Southampton, Cherbourg, Antwerp and the Hook of Holland are examples. Brussels has too its own fine international airport at Melsbroeck, and is a stopping place for trans-European express trains on many routes.

All this Leopold II of Belgium seems to have foreseen when he declared: 'Brussels can become the turntable of Europe.' It is not to be wondered at that the city has developed as a centre for European congresses and exhibitions and even for World Fairs. This manifold activity brings money into Brussels, and the civic authorities have been wide awake to their duty and opportunities in providing good conference halls, exhibition sites and hotels, and the Government in laying out around it a network of road and rail communications.

As you step down from your aircraft or your international train you will be certain to find the Brussels hostesses about you: those delightful, energetic, take-care-of-everything young women whose mission is to smooth the path of the bewildered new arrival. Their existence began as a mere bright idea, in connection with an exhibition in the city in 1958, but so valuable an asset have they been found, to a tourist centre like Brussels, that after the exhibition closed they were not, as had been expected, allowed to disband, and they have even increased in number and usefulness.

One might imagine at first sight that they are chosen solely for charm and good looks, but five minutes in the company of one shows that here you have a welcome, ready, practical help, oceans of information and even guidance, all in one compact and attractive bundle. They will take you in hand, but only as much as you want: find you an hotel, book you theatre tickets, produce a handful of leaflets on any subject connected with your stay, riffle through the complexities of a fat continental time-table and present you in seconds with the times of your train journey on to Bremen, Barcelona or Belgrade, neatly jotted down on a slip of paper, and tell you what you must see, how to shop and where to eat, in any part of their city.

In their shapely red jackets, with 'Brussels' in French on one shoulder and in Flemish on the other, their slim, navy blue skirts, spotless white blouses and gloves, with a dark tie and a jaunty tricorne hat, they will come hurrying to meet you, a smile of welcome on their lips and a neat blue sling bag swinging from one shoulder. You have only to ask for their help and it is freely given.

Some of the hostesses can always be found in the futuristic-looking information kiosk on the traffic island in the middle of place de Brouckère. Here they have batteries of telephones, mountains of directories and skyscrapers of filing cabinets, to enable them to help you. Their headquarters, in rue du Chêne, though, is still more worth a visit, situated as it is on the top floor of a very fine old burgher house. The rooms they occupy are what one could really call a magnificent garret. The glorious roof-timbers and arched doorways have been exposed; the furnishings are in keeping with the period, and there is a wonderful view down upon old Brussels from the numerous mullioned windows.

Brussels is often spoken of as 'Petit Paris', but though it is a city of light-hearted charm, there is an atmosphere too of something deeper and more enduring which gives it a very special place in the hearts of many. To them it is the best-loved of European capitals, even if it is smaller than most of them.

Chapter 2

Mirror to an Old City

THE glory of Brussels, and its centre, is the incomparable Grand' Place. If a visitor had, by unlucky chance, ten minutes only to spend in the city, he should stipulate for five of them to be spent in the Grand' Place in sunshine, and the other five after dark. Then he could take away with him a memory which would enable him to say, for the rest of his life: 'I have seen Brussels.'

Other cities in Belgium may have single treasures greater, or more beloved for this or that reason. The Gothic jewel boxes which are the town halls of Louvain and Oudenaarde call forth delighted cries from visitors; the sudden laughter of carillon music from the belfry of Bruges or the cathedral of Saint Rombaud, Malines (whose very name is a chime), can ring in the ears of those who love them but are far away; miracles in paint like the van Eyck brothers' triptych in Ghent, and Rubens's monumental 'Descent from the Cross' at Antwerp live in the mind's eye of many who can never hope to see them again. But the Grand' Place in Brussels has a unity and a completeness in its beauty which make it unlike anything else in Europe, if not in the world. You can stand at its centre and looking long at all its sides in turn see no single stone which strikes a discordant note.

Brussels began on its Grand' Place and the area most closely surrounding it. As long ago as the thirteenth century dwellers in the riverside village of Broecksele collected pebbles from their stream and laid them down to provide a patch of what is now called 'hard-standing' for the use of traders and stall-keepers carrying on the business of their very modest market. Each new

4

Grand' Place (for an enlargement of the area was required more than once) was laid on top of the old, so that the original square of cobbles is now buried nearly four feet below the granite setts of today.

Houses grew up around this 'Marct'; centuries passed and the one-time village became by degrees a wealthy and busy town. Civic pride in the Low Countries always finds very early expression in the building of an *hôtel de ville*, often so designed as to be in strong open rivalry with that of some other town. So it was in Brussels. Around the City Hall, girdling the vast square of today, there was a cordon of wooden houses in an assortment of styles. Old engravings still in existence give an idea of this happy hotchpotch of dwellings.

The left wing of the City Hall was added in the fifteenth century, but in less than a hundred years the hall was proving too small for its purpose. So the right wing was built, shorter of necessity since lack of space forbade its matching the earlier one. Where they joined, the magnificent Lion Staircase was built, and above it, as time went on, arose the magic of Jan van Ruysbroeck's delicate spire, soaring on and upward until the sixteen-foot gilded figure of Saint Michael, patron of the city, which forms its wind vane, is slaying the devil among the clouds.

The facade is a display of all that is best in Gothic: three floors of decorated, mullioned windows, and hundreds of statues, each in its own canopied niche. At every corner of the building rise octagonal pinnacles, each one three times encircled by a delicately wrought pierced stone gallery, and crowned by a crocketed spirelet. In the vast sweep of the roof are four rows of eighteen dormer windows, the dormers diminishing in size as they rise higher. The lovely main tower, square till it reaches roof level, then becomes six-sided, and rises in three diminishing tiers, each pierced by double-lighted windows, and decked with pinnacles like those on the main building. Topping all is a fretted spire through which the sky can be seen.

Within, the City Hall is full of beauty and dignity, and visitors
fortunate enough to be entertained to mid-morning champagne
by the Bourgemeester will certainly remember his stately parlour,
with its tapestries, paintings and statuary and the carefully chosen
period furniture. The general public can see at any time the
splendid Salle des Mariages, where, even if a religious ceremony
is also desired, every couple must attend for the legalization of
their union. Here again are fine carved panelling and tapestries,
rows of seats for the friends of bride and groom, and set out in
lonely state in front, looking very isolated in that vast emptiness,
their two large square stools, covered in rich, wine-red brocade.

If you are lucky enough to arrive when it is not in use—and
this of course applies equally to the Salle des Mariages—you may
see the reception chamber of the Echevin (Alderman) de l'Etat
Civil. Here you will receive a handshake from the white-haired
lady who conducts all these marriages, and whose proudest
boast it is that she married her king to his queen. Even they had
to attend there for the ceremony, and side by side before her
beautiful inlaid and gilded writing table are the red leather and
mahogany chairs which they used.

Come out now into the great square and feast your eyes upon
this glory of Flemish baroque architecture. In 1695 French troops
bombarded the Grand' Place until all its houses, with the exception of parts of two of them, were laid in ruin. The spire of
the City Hall, however, which throughout had provided the
target for the French batteries outside Brussels, remained un-
damaged. During the five years following the attack a miracle
of reconstruction was wrought: the thirty-three houses surrounding the Grand' Place were all restored by the trade gilds
whose headquarters they had been, and having been built within
so short a time are all of one period of architecture. Yet no two
are exactly alike.

The Grand' Place is often called, in casual speech, a square,
but it is not, being about twice as long as it is wide. The City

Hall occupies about two-thirds of one of the long sides, and on the other, set in the middle third, is the King's House; not so old, but in similar style. It is the home of the city museum. To the right and left of this are groups of gild houses, seven and six of them respectively, and five more stand beside the City Hall. On one short side of the Place there are seven houses, and facing them, eight. All have the most delicious names, such as The Fox Cub, The King of Spain, The Sack, The Wheelbarrow, Mount Tabor, Fame, Fortune, Joseph, Anne, The Tin Pot.

Friezes of sculptured figures, pierced stone balconies, rows of single statues, pediments, caryatids, sea-horses, tritons, festoons of fruit and flowers, all form parts of the decoration of this picture gallery of house-fronts. The architects of these façades, so diverse and yet so unified, gave imagination free rein here, at a period when building design was especially full of a happy exuberance. Many of the doorways are decorated with carvings of the tools used by the tradesmen to whose gild houses they give entry; and the beautiful gables have for their finials such varied motifs as a crown, a shell, an urn, a rearing lion. The entire gable of the House of the Boatmen takes the form of a Spanish galleon, complete with its high, balustraded stern-walk, and to look up at it for a few minutes against a background of flying clouds is to imagine it moving upon a restless sea. On the gable of the house known as The Golden Tree stands a colossal equestrian statue of Charles of Lorraine, the most popular of all the governors of the Netherlands. His outstretched right arm points away across the Place to the home on the Coudenberg Hill of his successors in rule, the Belgian royal family.

If you are to form in your mind's eye any picture of this lovely square, you need to add to it one more detail: that all its wealth of raised decoration on every one of the buildings around it, excepting only the vastly older Hôtel de Ville and King's House, is picked out in gold. The picture can be imagined, then, when

the whole is floodlit; and floodlighting is among the things that Belgians so well know how to do.

You pass through any one of a number of narrow streets— there are no wide ones—which lead to the Place, and you come, totally unexpectedly, into this conclave of golden frontages, all seeming to whisper together of the past, and to be tossing back at each other the light from a thousand pieces of gilding, glowing on the russet stonework of the varied façades. Only the City Hall and King's House, innocent of gold decoration, seem in the glow of the lights as if chiselled in old ivory, for Belgium does not make the common and ruinous mistake of using assorted colours in the floodlighting of ancient architecture.

Some of these fine houses, no longer gild headquarters, are now government and insurance offices, military and cultural clubs, banks and the like, but a few are cafés, and it is a good thing to take a cup of coffee in one of them, to see its ancient interior. Very often the first floor is more interesting than the street-level rooms. Two or three are antique and lace shops, and so there is easy entry.

At the left side of the City Hall, the first of the five gild houses is called De Sterre (The Star) and in the wall of this, just inside the narrow street between it and the Hôtel de Ville, is an interesting statue. In the fourteenth century Belgium—though it was not called that then—was under the rule of a powerful duke who died without a male heir. His two daughters were married and their husbands both wished to rule in the place of their father-in-law. The husband of the younger lost no time in marching on Brussels, and set up headquarters in the house called De Sterre on the Grand' Place. Enraged by this act, a citizen named Everard 't Serclaes tore down the invader's standard, and the burghers found so much courage from his boldness that they seized any weapons on which they could lay their hands and cleared the city of their enemy. The unfortunate Serclaes was, however, murdered a few days after, and his statue was later set up on the

The Grand'
Place has a
unity and
completeness
which make
it unique
(*page 4*)

Grand' Place . . . ' a picture gallery of house fronts ' (*page 7*)

The Salle des Mariages, Hôtel de Ville (*page 6*)

The King's House, Grand' Place (*page 7*)

The colossal statue of Charles of Lorraine on the gable of The Golden Tree in the Grand' Place points to the home on the Coudenberg Hill of his successors, the Belgian royal family (*page 7*)

The Oldest Citizen of Brussels, Manneken-Pis (*page 9*)

The City Hall by night (*page 5*)

Across a sheet of water the Parliament House faces the main entrance of the Parc de Bruxelles

On each of the pillars in the railings round the Jardin du Sablon stands a bronze figurine representing one of the trade gilds of Brussels (*page 10*)

The Cathedral of Saints Michael and Gudule

Few Belgians would consider the day complete without *biftek et frites* (*page 14*)

Frites are liberally bathed in mayonnaise, made on the premises (*page 14*)

wall of 'The Star' house. In a stone niche the dead Serclaes is half sitting, half lying, with his dog at his feet, and there seem always to be fresh flowers placed at his side. To touch the bared right arm of the figure, or the head of the dog, is supposed to bring good luck for the rest of the day. These two parts of the otherwise greenish group, which is in bronze, shine like gold from the constant touching of passers-by, and indeed are quite considerably worn away.

In a street very near here, named the rue de l'Etuve, lives that charmingly scandalous person, Manneken-Pis: the Oldest Citizen of Brussels, as he is always called.

The legend has it that a wealthy burgher of Brussels had a two-year-old son, who strayed from the house and was lost. There was a great hunt through all the streets of the city, and at last the father himself found the boy. Someone had stolen all his fine clothes and he was quite naked. But when his father found him, it is said at the same street corner where his statue stands today, he was laughing happily and wetting into the gutter. Another version of the legend—and there are heated supporters of both—declares that during a foreign occupation of Brussels the child stood at an upper window and in the same manner disrespectfully sprinkled an enemy officer in full uniform passing in the street below. Whichever is true, the child continues this performance today, not to mention his impish grin, and no doubt the ever-full fountain basin at his feet was a blessing to the district for washing floors and pavements in an age which knew nothing of taps and piped water in every home.

There is no very dependable record of when the statue was set up in its corner. Nowadays it is heavily railed off from inter-ference. The city is so fond of the boy—he somehow seems to be the embodiment of its good fortune—that he has been stolen on a number of occasions, mostly, it is supposed, by gangs from rival towns, but he is always as mysteriously returned, on some conveniently dark night. People's affection for Manneken-Pis

B

takes a very real form: several times he has been left money by will, and these sums are faithfully used for his upkeep: the painting of his railings and so on. He has a huge wardrobe of outfits, which is kept in a special room in the museum of the King's House on the Grand' Place (see page 55).

From many parts of Brussels the great Palace of Justice can be seen. It is the biggest building in Europe, larger than Saint Peter's in Rome, since it covers six and a half acres. If the visitor has the energy to climb the nearly six hundred steps to the dome, the reward will be a view over the greater part of the province of Brabant. Here, inside the great gilded crown on the top of the dome, are the transmitters of Eurovision.

From the Palais de Justice a very interesting walk can be taken, so planned as to include most of the historic sights of Brussels. The way leads at first along the fine, wide rue de la Régence, which runs in a direct line away from the main entrance to the Palais. The really exquisite Gothic church of Notre-Dame du Sablon (Our Lady of the Sandhill) is on the left of this street, and on the right a public garden of the same name contains a double statue of Counts Egmont and Hoorn. These two patriots are affectionately remembered to this day all over Belgium, with statues, street-names and so on. When, in the sixteenth century, the country was under the rule of Spain, her treatment of the people was such that the entire populace was soon in revolt. The infamous Duke of Alva received orders to 'drown this rebellion in blood'. One of his first acts was to behead the two most popular leaders in the country, Egmont and Hoorn. The scandal of their brutal execution in the Grand' Place at Brussels resulted in war.

The railings surrounding the Sablon garden are worthy of notice. Each stone pillar bears on its top a bronze figurine representing one of the trade gilds of Brussels. Count Egmont's palace stands just above the garden; it is converted now into government offices. Quite near here, too, is the former palace of the Thurn und Taxis family, who originated postal services in

Europe in 1460. For long they issued their own stamps, printed
with the family name.

Soon the royal palace of King Baudouin and Queen Fabiola
can be seen on the right, and in front of it, running parallel with
rue de la Régence for a long way, lies the Parc de Bruxelles, with
its fine trees, walks, lawns, fountains and statuary. Rue de la
Régence at this point becomes the rue Royale. It is interesting to
walk along inside the park railings, noting how wonderfully it is
surrounded by what Shakespeare called a 'pleached' fence: high
lime trees whose branches are painstakingly cut, trained and
intertwined to form a flat wall of living green. The brilliant flower-
beds are typical of Brussels park cultivation at its best.

The central avenue of the Parc comes out of it at the main
entrance, and the Palais de la Nation is then immediately opposite
the gates. This is the Belgian parliament house, and the interiors
of the fine buildings are shown daily, both those of the Senate and
the House of Representatives. These, particularly the great semi-
circular debating chamber of the Senate, have splendid paintings
and statuary.

A look to the right, up the long, straight rue de la Loi, before
leaving it for the forecourt of the parliament house, shows at the
top of a gradual rise the magnificent triple arch of the Cinquantenaire, spanning the roadway. This commemorates fifty years of
Belgian independence, and the triumphant air of the whole
quadriga on its top seems a fitting token of the national rejoicing at that time. In the opposite direction, the rue de la Loi
leads down to the cathedral of Saints Michael and Gudule, which
has been for centuries the country's national church. Everyone
visits this noble Gothic cathedral, to marvel over the stained glass
designed by the early sixteenth-century Flemish painter Bernard
van Orley.

There is one more place of pilgrimage for the visitor, farther
along the rue Royale. Here, on the left of it, stands the Colonne
du Congrès, which was erected to mark the first assembly of a

parliament of independent Belgium. On the top of the pillar is a statue of Leopold I and at its foot two huge standing lions in bronze. Between them lies Belgium's Unknown Warrior, with a perpetual flame leaping from a bronze basin at the foot of the grave. Around and behind the column there is slowly arising the great complex of buildings to be known as the Cité Administrative, where all the local government departments for Brussels will be centred.

If you go to stay in Brussels, ask someone to show you how to find the rue d'Une Personne. It is called this because it is so narrow that you can stand with a hand on each of its old grey walls; if two people wish to pass one of them must step into a doorway. As you stand there, call up the memory of the magnificent line of the broad rue de la Loi, sweeping up to the arch of the Cinquantenaire. Then contrast in your mind the figure of the oldest citizen of Brussels grinning down into his overflowing fountain basin with the splendid seraphic dignity on the young face of Saint Michael on the spire of the City Hall (there are many pictures of him in the shops).

Rue d'Une Personne; rue de la Loi. Michael the Archangel; Manneken-Pis. The alleys of Les Marolles and the stately mansions on the avenue Louise. Truly 'P'tit Paris' is a city of contrasts, especially in the things of the past. In the affairs and projects of tomorrow she has as much of interest and variety to offer.

Chapter 3

Fare and Square

No VISITOR to Brussels can help being struck by the number of cafés in the city; about every third or fourth building seems to be one. Like the Paris cafés, they do a good part of their business on the pavements; the same deep canvas awnings run the full length of their frontages, covering a wooden platform of the same area and three or four inches high, on which are set chairs and round tables with gaily coloured cloths. There will be a man-high glass screen at each end, discreetly separating the café premises from the neighbouring piece of pavement, which as likely as not belongs to another café.

Inside there will be eating-rooms both upstairs and down; maybe also in the more determinedly 'amusing' places, in the basement as well, and at least one source of music. This may be a mere juke-box, or an orchestra, with or without a solo singer or singing group. This depends upon the standing of the place.

The cafés have great variety of interesting names; why, one wonders, The Eleven Fish, The Golden Wheelbarrow, The Hopping Porter, The Angry Old Devil—of which two words are French and two are Flemish—and Slip-on? Throughout the day, though it is only in the evening that they ever appear really busy, there seem to be a few people at the tables, even from very early morning. If there is anyone at the table, cups or glasses will be on it, or coming in a moment, for the Belgians are great drinkers. This is most definitely not to say drunkards. Drunkenness is rarely seen, but the Belgian and his wife everywhere 'enjoy their glass' several times a day, and know what they want and choose it with care and intelligence.

13

The cafés, of course, exist mainly to supply coffee, though they keep a good variety of other drinks. Food to accompany them is in many places not available; in others the most that would be on offer is soup, or steak and chips. And here, with those last three magic words, one comes to a staple favourite of Belgians everywhere. *Biftek et Frites*: you cannot walk many yards in downtown Brussels without seeing the sign in window after window.

The *biftek* will be a large one, with a lump of melting butter on the top and plenty of *frites*, liberally bathed in mayonnaise. Few middle-class Belgians would consider the day complete without *biftek et frites* at least once, although the meat may occasionally be varied to a pork chop of generous proportions. The mayonnaise will have been lovingly made in the kitchen; to buy mayonnaise ready mixed in a branded bottle is the mark of the ignoramus.

The *frites*, in addition to being available at all hours in any café, can be had at a thousand and one street stalls in Brussels, and the aroma of them is so characteristic of the capital that the Bruxellois say that there should be no need for any radar aircraft direction when fog blankets Melsbroeck Airport.

A number of the cafés supply hot soup, and an excellent soup it will be. Anyone wanting a meal in a hurry asks for this at a café and eats his own sandwiches or other snack with it, following up with coffee or a beer. Cafés take no exception to the eating of one's own *pique-nique* in this way. For a proper meal the only place is a restaurant, though here the service is of necessity slower, since every dish is cooked especially for the customer, the practice of keeping food hot, ready to serve, being regarded with something like contempt.

Incidentally the catering at Belgian railway stations and the national airport and air terminals, available, of course, to the general public, is really outstandingly good. The traveller will gratefully recall memorably good breakfasts eaten in the under-

ground concourse at the heart of the newly built Gare Centrale at
Brussels. Across the road is the terminal building of Sabena, the
national airline, and here a lunch of fruit juice, clear soup, smoked
salmon, roast duck and new peas, topped off with gooseberry
tart and cream and an almost intimidating array of cheeses,
lingers in my memory, though it was in no way outside routine
for the airline's restaurant.

The Belgian, and the Bruxellois in particular, sets no store
by any sort of hurried snack; he prefers to sit down to 'square
fare', a good and carefully chosen meal, with plenty of hot, rich
food, and plenty of time given to enjoying it.

The coffee served, unless *café au lait* has been especially asked
for, will be *un filtre*, but in either case very good. The *filtre* consists of an electro-plated individual stand, holding its own lidded
coffee container with a perforated bottom, poised over an empty
cup on a matching tray. Boiling water is poured on to the coffee
and the whole brought to the table, and over a cigarette
the customer watches the filtered coffee drip slowly into his cup
and then adds milk and sugar to his liking. A good deal of chicory
is used with the coffee; most Belgians like its bitter taste.

Of beers there are numerous varieties, some as pale and innocent as a soft drink and delightfully refreshing, others with a
swift and determined power, which may or may not be immediately apparent. Since beer is really the national drink it is
not surprising that the country has made every possible effort
to keep alive its dozens of lesser brewing firms by means of
taxation concessions. There is one old and highly honoured type
of beer named Faro, which has been brewed by the same methods,
it is reliably said, for just over a thousand years.

There are no vineyards in Belgium, but the pick of French and
other wines finds its way to the shops of Brussels; very good ones
are even to be seen racked on the shelves of self-service stores,
and expected by the very ordinary housewife to be there. Wheeled
shopping-baskets weave to and fro on the pavements in their

scores; these are not so much an indulgence for the lazy as a
necessity. Housewives throughout Belgium insist on choosing
their own goods; few would dream of relying on a telephoned
and delivered order. Full use is made by them of the street
markets, where dealers in country produce appear daily with their
own wares, bringing a vastly increased quantity and a wider
selection on a Saturday. The middle-class Brussels shopper, therefore, will return from a visit to the shops or market laden with
groceries and provisions, fruit, *salades*, wine, vegetables, even
cleaning and washing materials, all personally selected. Having
in all probability a large family who will certainly be hearty
eaters, she needs to buy generously, and packs her useful push-
basket to its limit.

What should the visitor taste who wants to feel he has really
sampled Brussels food? The rue des Bouchers (Butchers' street)
in the old town is a street almost entirely of restaurants, and some
of these are specialized seafood places of very high standard,
but all sorts of eating-houses can be found without ever having,
in any part of Brussels, to walk more than a few yards.

Waterzooie, whose name sounds so sadly more diluted than the
delectable reality, covers a variety of very well made soups: in
Brussels the most usual kinds are fish or chicken, mingled with a
number of cleverly flavouring herbs and vegetables. With his
frites the Bruxellois adores mussels, and these can be very good
indeed, though there must be an R in the name of the month for
them to be available. A few restaurants boast of being able to
cook them in as many as twenty-eight different ways. But the
unwary visitor should be warned: the Belgian being such a redoubtable eater, the visitor ordering *moules et frites* will be con-
fronted with a bowl of these delicacies as big across and half as
deep as a kitchen bucket.

Tomates aux crevettes (tomatoes hollowed out and refilled with
a savoury mixture of shrimps and mayonnaise) is a favourite
dish everywhere which all visitors should try, and the variety of

boudins seems inexhaustible. *Boudin* is a common term for a sausage, and Belgian sausages can be of all sizes, from a private enterprise matter for consumption by one person only to a large and sturdy affair, long enough and corpulent enough to supply half a dozen households. They can be pink, cream-coloured, bright red, white, speckled or black. When black and white are served together, and this is a very popular choice, they are called *ciel et terre*.

Brussels knows all there is to know about using odd and unexpected flavourings, and, with the Forêt de Soignes on her very outskirts, game is abundant. So hares are cooked with prunes, and roots and berries such as chervil and juniper are used in pickling hams. Cod is delicately poached in a mixture of lemon juice and beef extract.

Fruit, as a glance at shop windows and street stalls will confirm, is abundant and of wonderful quality. Belgium's own plums in late summer are of staggering size and of a lovely golden-red colour.

Brussels is outstanding as a production centre for fancy cakes and pastries, and its ices, sweets and chocolates are memorable. Many of the luxury shops produce hand-made chocolates with a variety of exotic fillings, flavoured to order—'especially for M. and Mme X, who like this mingling of lime and cucumber'. Or it may be of bitter orange and mint, or some other highly personal combination. Ices can be had in dozens of flavours, even including beer. Nougat is outstandingly popular, and entire street-stalls are devoted to its sale, prewrapped in blocks running up to a handsome size.

Having had a long-standing association with Africa, Belgium produces excellent slab chocolate; in Brussels a brand to look out for, fine-flavoured and in milk or plain blends—the latter being known as fondant—is Côte d'Or, with its familiar trade mark of the golden elephant and two palm trees.

Chapter 4

'Quartier Populaire'

BRUSSELS, like most other cities, has its picturesque and crowded 'populaire' quarter, and the best view over this area can be had from quite close to the Palais de Justice, which appears, by contrast with what one is looking down upon, an almost overwhelmingly majestic building.

Make for the place Poelaert, and stand facing the tremendous main façade of the Courts of Justice. To the right you will notice that place Poelaert stands, as it seems, on the edge of space, with the usual city haze rising from the abyss, and a stone balustrade to prevent you from falling over into it. Beyond this is a mosaic of roof-tops, gables, windows and chimneys, with here and there the loom of great trees in public parks, short stretches of street and railway, Saint Michael on his spire topping the Hôtel de Ville, and away to the right the twin towers of the cathedral. Gleaming in the middle distance is the bubble-dance of the nine silver spheres of the Atomium, and about as far away again, if it is a clear day, the royal church of Laeken can be seen rising from trees which plume the distant ridge, with that curious house of cards, the Chinese Pavilion, in the palace grounds, seeming to be quite near to it.

But it is the immediate foreground to the view from the balustrade that is of importance now, for from here, better perhaps than from anywhere else in Brussels, it can be seen that the city is built upon two levels. The stone barrier is more than roof-high to even the tallest of the buildings in that part of the old town lying immediately below it. Views through windows and

18

down into courts and alleys can be had from here as from nowhere else. Here a class of children in one of the state secondary schools apply themselves to their books; there a typist sits in a stuffy back office, her fingers performing a spirited dance, soundless at this distance, over the keys of her machine; in a yard an old man breaks firewood; along some narrow cobbled alley a hawker of *caricoles* (black-shelled whelks) pushes a barrow close to a kerbside, his shout perceptible only as a cavern in his florid face.

The traveller who investigates this quarter will find it one of the most animated in Brussels—Les Marolles.

This area stretches from the place de la Chapelle—very nearly in the centre of the ancient heart-shaped city—to the porte de Hal, a medieval gateway on the inner ring road, where the highway from Waterloo enters the city of today. At the place de la Chapelle there is an interesting street market, and the great tower of the church of La Chapelle looks down upon the many stalls here set out, mainly of food and cheap clothing. Within the church is buried the painter Pieter Breughel the Elder, whose home at 132 rue Haute, on the way into Les Marolles from place de la Chapelle, has one of a number of attractive and interesting old gables to be seen in this quarter.

Rue Haute, and rue Blaes parallel to it, both run directly through this part of Brussels from end to end. They are joined by narrow alleys, and between these and on the outer sides of the two main arteries are many culs-de-sac, steep, cobbled and sunless, even none too salubrious, it might seem. Towering over every one in turn as the passer-by peeps into it from the left side of either of the two chief streets—going towards the ring boulevard—is the frowning cliff of the Palais de Justice.

The older Marolliens have no great love for the Palais de Justice, and that is quite apart from its main function. Did it not destroy, in its own birth, a good part of their quarter? Even the big red-brick blocks of tenements, built as a part of the first attempts at slum clearance between the wars for the housing of their own sons and daughters, are not over-popular. Nor is the still later extension of the large and efficient hospital in their midst, centuries ago a *léproserie* of the same name: Saint Peter's. After all, who can possibly regard the comforts of a hospital bed, in the wholly unlikely event of a broken leg, as compensation for the sweeping away of Black Swan Court over there, and the compulsory rehousing, in one of those red-brick barracks of *appartements sociales*, of all its people: the Bogart family, Grandmother Malpas, who was so happily rooted in her one tiny room, the Desprez, the Moulins, blind Madame Vlaminck and so many more? It was all kinds of a pest, that. . . . It seems not unnatural that one of the Marollien's most venomous terms of abuse, if he becomes involved in a street brawl, is 'Architek'.

Here then lives the Marollien in all the mystery of his strange separateness from the life of the city so close around him; his limited range of trade and calling; his rough jollity; his strong spirit of loyalty to other dwellers 'op de Marolle', as he will put it.

The name of the quarter, originally settled in the fourteenth century by an influx of Walloon workers from outer Brabant, is derived from a convent of Apostolines Maricoles in the neighbourhood, whose name of Maricoles came in its turn from the Latin 'colere Mariam'—to honour Mary. Its people, now Marolliens for generations, may be street hawkers, errand boys, door-to-door pedlars, unskilled labourers, window-cleaners, market porters, rag-dealers. To satisfy their needs, the two main streets of the area are lined with flashy and overcrowded shops for the sale of cheap clothing, garish furniture, carpets and lampshades, plastic flowers and ornaments, pictures in hard colourings and frames of still harder hues. Much of this trash crowds the pavements, and the sound of noisy radios pours from steamy eating-houses along with their rich and spicy smells.

The Marolliens speak a language of their own, which is a mingling of Flemish and Spanish. Though it is on the way out, this patois still provides a florid and useful selection of invective and terms of abuse. At one time there were frequent and blood-stained battles between the dwellers in Les Marolles and those of adjoining districts, but these are now rare, and the visitor wishing to see this interesting quarter can do so alone or in company, in perfect safety, with fear neither for himself nor for his belongings.

In Les Marolles is a strong feeling of *zwanze*, an untranslatable term which combines love of the home territory with loyalty to those who dwell there. This shows itself in the instant adoption of any *pauvre gosse* who finds himself or herself motherless. Large families are the rule, and homes are crowded: there are a couple of rooms at the most. But one more mouth to feed—what is that, when there are already so many? The home is even now bursting at the seams? Well, but life is lived mostly in the streets in any case, when the weather allows.

Poverty is the normal condition. But each court or street, housing half a dozen to twenty families, is a tightly knit community. First Communion of young Jean-André or Bernadette next week? A stiff black suit and white gloves, a long white dress and flowing veil, in which Jean-André will look like an old man at a funeral and Bernadette like a miniature bride, are *de rigueur*. But all that costs money. Jean-André and Bernadette, however, must not be put to shame in the eyes of the next alley. So the street has always its communal *tenue* (outfit) *de Première Communion*, both for boy and girl, though the fact is supposed to be a secret. Out it comes; a hem on a too-long trouser is tacked up; a tuck is let down on a white satin skirt, and all is well.

Even the Bruxellois is sometimes surprised to find that, should he go seeking a certain dweller in Les Marolles, quite near neighbours do not at first know him or her. There is no pretence about this, either. The new arrival is wanting, perhaps, to trace Madame Legros, having heard a rumour in the world outside (two or three streets away) that she has a child's push-chair for sale. He approaches a large and unshapely old lady dozing on the pavement in a backless, rush-seated chair.

'Do you know where I can find Madame Legros? I have been told that she lives here.'

('Here' may be a court of half a dozen houses.)

A vague grunt, a screwing up of watery old eyes, a mumbling at toothless gums, the shaking of a wispy grey head.

'*Hein?* . . . Madame Legros? . . . Madame—What is it? . . . Legros? . . . Madame Legros. . . . *Non, non,* I do not know such a one.'

'I am sure it was here they said she lives. They told me she has a child's push-chair for sale.'

'*Oé.* . . . Ah. . . . But certainly, yes. . . . Good enough. . . . That is my son's married daughter. My grand-daughter Mariette, of course. . . . It is that house, over the road.'

The old lady is asleep again almost before her pointing arm falls. But she has had time to reflect briefly on the oddness of strangers. . . . Grand-daughter Mariette, now; who could be expected to know that her name was Madame Legros?

Do not leave Les Marolles, whatever you do, without a visit to its 'Flea Market', one of the sights of Brussels, and an essential expedition for all who want to know a remarkable facet of this city. Do not at all let yourself be dismayed by its name; though there may be many dirty old things to be seen in this market, you will catch nothing but the spirit of the place.

Sunday morning is its best and busiest time; after, perhaps, you have been to enjoy the music of the Mass at the cathedral of Notre-Dame du Sablon. Make your way along the rue Haute until you see a turning rue des Renards on your right. This leads into the place du Jeu de Balle, a large open square. Here, surrounded by a milling multitude, you will find stalls for the sale of everything imaginable: broken-down clocks and worn-out car tyres; boots and ball-pens, pre-war gramophones and their records; bird-cages and washing-machines; glass, copper, brass and ironware; second-hand tools and sewing-machines; magazines, books; pictures framed and unframed; tailors' dummies, dented brass band instruments; prams, rusty oil-stoves and string-less violins; items of broken harness, sheet music, obsolete gas-light fittings, guitars, pocket torches, mantelpiece ornaments, linoleum and fire-irons. Most of these things will be very much more than second-hand, but some few may be new. Here you can buy buttons and bootlaces, penknives and pickle jars, stockings and screwdrivers. Here you will see waist-high mounds of old locks, of keys of every size, of nuts and bolts, of battered shoes, of chair-springs, gloves and radio parts.

Keep your eye on the bric-à-brac stalls. A bargain is far less likely now than it would have been twenty years ago, but it is still possible. Perhaps I may be allowed to record two which have come my way. I discovered on one such stall an eighteenth-century lidded drug jar, in blue and white Delft, made for the shop of some long-departed chemist, with a charming cartouche of cross and angels on its front, surrounding the word 'Wermod' (Wormwood). Five years later I came upon its twin, labelled for 'Moschus' (Musk). And the price had suffered no increase in the interval.

The second story is taller, but no less true. At home I had bought, for a song because it had lost its stopper, a deep-blue Bristol glass flagon with a silver collar and lip. It took about twenty minutes, in the Flea Market, to find a silver stopper, a trifle battered, but bearing the same beaded pattern round its top.

Argue a bit about the price of anything you fancy; you might even take the risk of turning away regretfully. You are quite likely to be called back.

Chapter 5

Fun and Games

TWICE within living memory Belgium has been overrun by an enemy, in the two greatest wars in history. Twice within living memory her capital has been occupied by German forces. In spite of, or perhaps because of, these bitter memories, the Belgian, and not least the Bruxellois, has preserved his almost medieval love of fun, robust play and a good carnival.

All these can be seen and enjoyed by the visitor to Brussels, provided he is there at the right time, and for the most characteristic of these pleasures the right time is nearly every evening, except Sundays.

Several towns in Belgium have marionette theatres, but the most renowned of them all was that of Toone, at Brussels. It was certainly in existence in the early eighteenth century, and the last Toone, with whose death the theatre unfortunately came to an end, was Toone VI. The Toone Theatre, with all its miniature actors, some of them ancient and very valuable, is now to be preserved in its entirety as a museum piece. There are several other old and new marionette theatres in Brussels: the Peruchet, the Théâtre des Cœurs de Bois and the Fauchonnet are among them, and at these similar performances can be seen regularly.

It is an interesting experience, if entry can be gained—it is not easy—to visit the Entreprises De Ryk, where puppets for all over Belgium are made. The visitor will see the wide range of these engaging figures which the factory produces, all by hand-work: soldier, monk, king, queen, judge, gipsy, devil, witch, bride, assassin, wicked uncle, coachman, dragon, pirate, abbot, ghost, jester and many more.

The traditional Brussels marionette is a rod-puppet, worked by a stiff wire passing through its head and ending in a handle for the manipulator. Being about the height of a five-year-old child, it is often of considerable weight. This applies especially to one favourite figure of a knight in full armour, whose 'dress material' consists of over sixteen hundred metal pieces. The forearms are moved by almost invisible wires, and the legs bend only at the hip. In spite of this the highly trained manipulators produce an amazing precision and grace of movement, and such is the illusion of reality in this minuscule world that when at the end of a performance the house lights go up one's fellow members of the audience seem suddenly of an incredible massiveness and to have the clumsiness of a herd of elephants when they leave their seats.

Stage properties, too, are cleverly contrived: one of my own memories is of a pair of roisterers who sat down at a table outside an inn, summoned the apple-cheeked serving-maid and ordered wine. Returning to the inn, she brought it out, poured it into the tall glasses in an audibly trickling red stream, and stood watching as the two visitors drained their glasses into their wooden throats.

Toone's theatre was at place de la Chapelle, in Les Marolles. There was not the comfortable seating one associates with a theatre; it was a converted wine-cellar behind an *estaminet*, with lime-washed walls and a vaulted ceiling, and accommodating a hundred and twenty people at most (and at a pinch) on wooden benches. The audience, a cross-section of the people of Brussels, was nearly as interesting as the show itself.

And what a playbill: cloak-and-dagger melodrama of every kind, freely adapted history of Belgium, fairy-tale and folklore, thrills of the French Revolution, Napoleon in exile, the Spanish Inquisition, Lucifer and his devils, the Four Sons of Aymon,

c

stories of dungeons and poisoners, runaway matches and hidden
treasure and every sort of derring-do. The *chef-d'œuvre* of Toone's
repertoire, *The Hunchback*, was billed as being 'in five acts and
twenty-seven tableaux' and as including 'four duels, two rapes,
two elopements and three murders'.

At the end of some of the more dramatic scenes barons would
have raged, women would have wept, heads would have rolled
and the stage be littered with corpses. But of one thing the spec-
tator could rest assured: vice would in the end be punished and
virtue rewarded; the oppressed and innocent maiden would recover her gold and regain her lover and the wicked uncle would
die horribly. All these conditions apply equally to the remaining
théâtres des marionettes; one can always guess just how every story
will end, yet in spite of that every story is of consuming interest!

A minor difficulty at these theatres is the language, for most
of the plays are presented in the patois of Les Marolles. In
addition they contain many comments on Brussels affairs and
personalities which the outsider cannot be expected to under-
stand. But the marionette theatre everywhere has a charm of its
own, and here, where it has been a part of life for so many generations, even the language barrier can be no serious hindrance to
enjoyment. It is a remarkable fact that in a city where theatre
'in the live', concert, cinema, ballet and circus (which last all
Belgium adores) are available with their superior resources as
entertainment, these miniature shows with their wooden actors
keep their public, its loyalty and patronage unimpaired.

It is fairly certain that those who, with such beautiful skill,
practise le Tir à l'Arc in Brussels will not find it easy to for-
give me for putting them under the heading of 'Fun and Games'.
I shall certainly offend again when I deal in this same chapter
with the Arbalétriers, so it might be well now to ask pardon of
both, and make my excuses.

These are sports, but unlike most other sports they have their
origin in a stern and ever-present necessity of the distant past.

The archers of Belgium are the present-day inheritors of a great tradition: the reincarnations of those strong arms, those unerring eyes, those courageous spirits, which built their nation in the past and defended it repeatedly from its enemies. What is more, they are proudly and constantly aware of that fact.

The very names of their ancient corporations are like a fanfare of trumpets. The Archers of Brussels, for example, are 'Le Grand Serment Royal des Archers de Saint Sébastien', and were founded in 1381. The Arbalétriers (Crossbowmen) are 'L'Ancien Grand Serment Royal et Noble des Arbalétriers de Notre-Dame du Sablon', founded in 1213.

Go and see, if you can, either or both of these Serments (the word means 'oath', but its nearest equivalent is, I suppose, the term 'Company' as it is applied to the London livery gilds) at their work. With that last word perhaps I make some amends for putting these reincarnated medieval defenders among the fun and games. Their performance is skilled, beautiful and exacting; it is the onlooker who will gain the enjoyment.

Both gilds meet at *estaminets* of ancient lineage, for both skills are thirsty work. The Archers can be found 'at the Sign of Saint John Baptist' in the rue de Laeken, and if you are lucky you may be allowed to handle one of the man-high bows, an arrow or two and an arm-guard of heavy leather.

Three or four contestants stand at the butts together. Notice their beautiful carriage and stance, the long, steady look measuring the distance, the absence of all sound. There is a moment of almost agonizing silence as they take aim, and then all four arrows are gone with a booming twang, and before the eye can follow the flight of even one there are four sharp thuds, making almost a single sound, on the targets mounted against a background of plaited straw at the far end of the range. Without a word the archers walk forward, each man down a separate 'alley', to recover their arrows, and disappear behind the scenes to mark up their scores. At the tables beside the range tension relaxes;

drinks are being served, and triumphs, past, present and hoped-
for, are the subject of conversation.

'Kingship' of the Archers, as of the Arbalétriers, is contested
annually, and a 'king' three years in succession becomes an
'emperor'. The company, like that of the Crossbowmen, possesses valuable treasure: prize silver tankards; a visitors' book
with signatures worth a fortune to collectors; the ancient charter
of the Serment with all its strict rules; the president's ceremonial
gold collar; the goblet he drains on nomination. At the headquarters of the Archers hang the portraits of all the 'kings'.
Every picture but one on the walls is riddled with arrow-holes,
for it is the custom at the end of the reign of each 'king' to use
his portrait as a target in a special match.

Both Serments enjoy royal patronage, and a patronage which
is no empty form, for members of the royal family visit the
companies regularly and honour them in other ways.

The Arbalétriers are, if possible, even more romantic. In
the rue des Visitandines, quite near to the church of La Chapelle,
is the charming old Estaminet des Visitandines which has
established itself in a disused convent of the Brigittines. Perhaps
that fact explains why, in the centre of a crowded city, it has a
large and delightful garden, with lichen-grown walls, an abun-
dance of flowers, a well and several fine trees. From the back
courtyard an outside staircase climbs to a loft which is the
Serment's treasure house and business meeting-place.

The Arbalétriers are devotees of the cumbersome and exacting
crossbow, which can kick like a mule on discharge, and whose
weight makes balancing it vertically on the shoulder feel like
upending a wheelbarrow. The 'bowstring' is not a string at all
but a strong metal rod, which can only be drawn back with
mechanical assistance, the 'bow' portion taking all the bend and
the rod none. The waist-high weapon is then elevated from the
shoulder and sighted on a mock bird made of wool, tinsel and
feathers, fluttering in the wind at the top of a hundred-foot pole.

A tense moment again, as pressure on the trigger increases, and then, with a sudden shock of sound like the slam of a car door, the ammunition—a light-alloy, spherical bullet three-quarters of an inch across—is let fly by the powerful spring, and with good aiming and some luck the moving 'bird' is smitten into fragments.

In some of the less busy streets of Brussels you come upon the *jeu de balle* (pelota) in progress. It looks much like tennis, but the net is set higher and the ball is larger and harder and the play faster. This is to be expected, for the racket is made of solid wood. An excited crowd will be found lining the pavements, and traffic must go round the block, out of the way.

Brussels is a city of pigeon-racers, and contests are arranged from as far away as Spain. It is an amusing sight to see an entire family hanging out of the top window of a house trying to coax some newly arrived star of the racing world back to its loft. Every kind of endearment, yell, whistle, coo, curse and merely curiosity-arousing noise is tried, while the cause of all the trouble sits with cool and maddening disregard upon some inaccessible wall or branch surveying the view and wasting precious minutes of clocking time.

The city dearly loves a procession, by which is meant a full-scale and wholly genuine *manifestation folklorique*, of which Belgium has a great many. These bring to life some historic, biblical or legendary story, and expand it into a grand cortège, in which personages of the past, kings, lawgivers, warriors, scriptural and religious characters, Moses, Samson, David and Goliath, with monks, abbots, bishops, devils and angels, creations of fantasy, witches, dragons, serpents, and even giants whose heads are level with the upper windows, parade in company with bands, gilds, corporations and standard-bearers.

Of these processions the most renowned in Brussels is the Ommegang which takes place in July, and amounts to a *résumé* of the history of the city, liberally and happily mixed with snippets of folklore from all over the country. It originally celebrated the arrival in the city of the statue of the Virgin of the Sablon, who is the patron saint of the Arbalétriers.

Here you will see, then, the fifteen Brussels giants, many of them of great age, including Mieke, Janneke and Saint Gudule, and another, even larger, Messire Jean de Nivelles. Of necessity all wear skirts, whether they represent men or women, and the voluminous draperies are the covering for a tent-shaped basket frame, in which walks the man carrying the giant, who sees where he is going through a square of black net inserted in the front of the skirt. The giants are weighty, and the walker inside the stuffy skirt will get regular relief.

There are also tableaux and moving groups put on by various corporations: the Arbalétriers and Archers, and such gilds as those of the Brewers, River Fishermen, *jeu de balle* players, cyclists, firemen and footballers, all carrying their banners. Here too are groups representing the different boroughs which make up Brussels, with statues of saints from their respective churches, and dramatization of any legends connected with them. Throughout the Ommegang the aristocracy of the city may in many cases be found enacting the parts of their own ancestors, who have figured in the past history of Brussels.

On Whit Monday comes the procession of Saint Guidon, whose church is in the suburb of Anderlecht. The saint, originally a farmer's boy, is the patron of coachmen, and of draught-horses generally. So all the horse-drawn transport of Brussels, which is of course growing less as the years pass, gathers in the Grand' Place, and accompanied by riders in hunting pink and a series of tableaux recounting the saint's life, moves off to Anderlecht. Outside the church the animals are blessed and they then march three times round it.

Chapter 6

Reporting for Duty

BRUSSELS enjoys work as well as play. Many writers of guide-books and travelogues on Belgium as a whole have used expressions as strong as 'zest for work and play' and 'attacking both work and play with gusto' when speaking of the people. Brussels is no exception.

'Work' for the Bruxellois begins at the age of six and at the hour of 8.15 a.m. At this time all the State schools, of which there is a very fine national system, start their day; many shops and offices open even earlier. There are a number of denominational schools, run by the religious communities, for both boys and girls, and these schools are subject to the government scheme of inspection.

Beginning compulsory education at six years of age, the child remains in the *primaire* grade until fourteen, when he can leave school if his parents so desire. Boys who stay on beyond this age continue in an Athénée and girls at a Lycée. The next stage is an Ecole Normale for those wanting teacher-training, and an Ecole Professionnelle for those seeking a course to fit them for business life or for trades; these courses include wood and metal work, electro-technology, typing and office routine, dressmaking, draughtsmanship, domestic science and the like. Those wishing to go on to a university do so from the Athénée or the Lycée.

The State schools, in Brussels as elsewhere, receive pupils of all shades of religious opinion, and doctrinal instruction up to two hours weekly is available in any denomination according to family choice. The University of Brussels, however, is described as *Libre*, having no religious bias. It now has fine buildings and an extensive campus, dating from between the wars, in the Ixelles district. It is extremely proud of its very modern and highly equipped School of Languages, where by means of the most modern equipment a native teacher of the language in question can deal with twenty or thirty students at once, causing them to read, or write to dictation in such a way that no pupil hears any other voice but his own and the teacher's.

In the newer suburbs on the city's fringe fine kindergarten, primary and secondary schools have sprung up since the end of the war, and there are also in most communes schools of art, music and technology, training colleges and numerous evening courses for the further education of adults. There is a nation-wide public library system, reaching remote districts by means of mobile libraries. The public library service in Brussels is particularly good and the buildings plentiful, modern and attractive.

It takes no visitor very long, even if he is among the chronically hard up, to discover that Brussels is a shopper's paradise. Possibly it is the visitor who has least to spend who will find this out most quickly, since the greater part of his shopping will have to be done from the outer side of the plate-glass window. Brussels is certainly worthy to rank beside any far bigger city, in America or Europe, in respect both of quality and choice of what is offered.

Except for a handful of chain and department stores, the shops of Brussels are not large, but for the most part discreetly middle-sized. All the city, and many people far outside it, know La Pléiade. For this is a group of Brussels shops, twenty-one in number, of each of which it can be said that in its line it cannot be bettered. Situated very roughly in a wide-flung oval about the Royal Palace and the Parc de Bruxelles, though one is as far afield as the suburb of Anderlecht, they all display the insignia of La Pléiade: seven stars within a circle and a crown above. The group says of itself that it has chosen a name which corresponds not so much to the number of its members as to their intentions. La Pléiade is the royal family of Brussels shops; there is no higher honour than to be elected to its register. It seems a pity to rob the members, by translation into English, of the beautiful restraint of the French 'labels' which each gives to himself on its pages. In alphabetical order of their owners' names there are 'tailleurs'; 'fournisseur de la Cour (vins et champagne)'; 'optique'; 'parfums et Institut de Beauté'; 'coiffure'; 'Le Fleuriste' —and what a difference the omission of the definite article would make here! Then comes the proud designation 'joaillier et orfévrier du Roi et de la Reine', and the list goes on with 'fourrure'; 'luminaires'; 'lingerie boutique'; 'décors et objets anciens'; 'chocolatier-confiseur'. Here it is worth pausing a moment to point out that not only in this establishment, but in most others where good chocolates may be had in Brussels, the proprietor is likely to faint quietly away if asked for 'a box of chocolates'. For this is the city of delicately flavoured miracle chocolates lovingly made by hand, and their providers expect them to be chosen individually with the same loving care: two or three of these, three or four of those, five of the other. They are expensive, but of the best. To buy carelessly, 'by the boxful', is the mark of one who knows nothing.

The constellation of La Pléiade continues with 'décorateur'; 'pâtissier-glacier'; 'garniture de table'; 'antiquaire'; 'couture'; 'haute mode'; 'chemisier (fournisseur de la Cour Royale)'; 'restaurant'—a very far cry, this, from the illuminated signs offering *Frites* on the street corners of Les Marolles!— and ends with 'imprimeur du Roi'. This last can proudly add: 'fondé en 1757', and completes the roll of these aristocrats of Brussels commerce.

La Pléiade publishes an extremely witty brochure about itself and its members, for free distribution; if you see its black-and-gold star-sprinkled cover anywhere it is well worth possessing. Each firm has a page to itself, on which its name and address appear below a very funny cartoon, the hero of every one of which is a scared-looking stocky man in a sola topee and safari kit, with or without his glamorous wife. In one he is struggling on his back, knife in hand, beneath the ravening jaws of a furious leopard, while the lady hides behind a cactus, and he gasps out to her: 'Darling, are you sure you wouldn't rather have a ready-made coat?' In another she follows him through dense jungle and declares: 'I'm sure I only brought along just the strictest necessities!' while behind them come two coolies with a pole on their shoulders on which hang about twenty coat-hangers adorned with sumptuous fur coats and evening dresses.

Of course Brussels has shops of all classes and kinds. In considering the variety of occupations open to the Bruxellois, one must therefore think of the multiplicity of things the city and neighbourhood can produce, thus providing work: food of all sorts, fine jewellery, clothing, furniture, glass, lace, china, flowers, industrial diamonds. The cream of the production of many other countries is available too: Italian footwear; French perfumes, gloves and enamels; Danish porcelain; Japanese pearls; Indian and Chinese ivories; Persian carpets; Swiss clocks and watches; American cars and cameras.

If you are not tied down to 'doing' the ordinary tourist sight-seeing of Brussels in a week, it is worth seeking out some of the activities of industry. Space allows only the suggestion of two or three at random; a letter to the public relations officer of the enterprise concerned will usually result in an invitation to see what is going on behind a many-windowed wall of brick, or a pair of discreetly closed double doors leading to an unassuming looking courtyard.

At Forest-lez-Bruxelles is a large factory bearing the sign Diamant-Boart and a figure of Saint Eligius, the patron saint of smiths. Try to see it if you can. Here are machines cutting, shaping, mounting and testing for hardness that invaluable aid to many modern industries: boart, the industrial diamond. The colour of the diamond boart matters not at all. While the gem-seeker has his vocabulary of romantic terms reminiscent of an artist's palette—blue-white, silver cape, fine cape, jonquil, gold-tawny—all that is demanded by the workers at avenue du Pont de Luttre in Forest are those inherent diamond qualities: hardness, resistance to great heat, accuracy of structure. Curiously enough, soft substances such as rubber, even cheese, are resistant to a diamond, but the hardest granite known succumbs. It is only now, with its rapidly increasing use as an industrial aid, that the world can fully appreciate the force of the name given to it at the opening of the Christian era by the naturalist Pliny: 'adama'—the untamable.

Brussels is a great city for family businesses, and in some cases the fifth and sixth generation in a direct line is carrying on the business today. An instance of this can be found in rue des Capucins, which is in Les Marolles. Here is the Etablissement de Backer et Fils: Fabrique de Passementerie.

Throughout Belgium, France, Luxembourg and Western Germany there is a great love of *passementerie* as a part of house-hold decoration. It can best be described as a glorified and elaborated version of the silk girdle and froggings on a man's dressing-gown. Windows are a great source of pride to the Belgian householder, and are enriched by beautiful curtains and draped pelmets, with heavily looped festoons of three, four and five silk cords terminated by thick tassels, and decorated with bunches and swags of highly realistic flowers, fruits, leaves and berries, made in the finest natural silk, using an ordinary sewing-needle only. Colour schemes are enchanting and trails of these flowers and leaves will be twined round mirrors and hung from chandeliers.

In rue des Capucins a dark red door leads through a narrow passage to a paved courtyard with a laburnum tree. In the win-dows all round the court can be seen the spinning-frames of the workers. The present Mr de Backer, sixth of his line, will show with pride examples of the work of his house, many pieces of which now hang in royal palaces. He will point to portraits of those who have gone before him in producing these miracles in natural silk imported from Italy and the Far East.

As you pass along the rue d'Arenberg your eye will be caught by a line of windows belonging to a goldsmith. The firm has a long and resounding history.

In 1840 one Louis Wolfers set off from Brussels on a two-year tour of France, wandering from workshop to workshop to pick up the lore of the goldsmith. This was so common a practice that he seems to have kept no record of his route, or of those who helped him. After his return he registered his master-engraver's *poinçon*: a design of a letter 'W' surmounted by a boar's head. That mark, on a recessed, barrel-shaped ground, is one of the most honoured and familiar in Belgium today.

Louis and his family worked originally in rue des Longs Chariots, at first solely by hand, but later, with the increasing pressure of the Industrial Revolution, with some help from machines. Such an innovation was strenuously resisted by the older craftsmen in their employ, who clung fiercely to the hand-made tradition. However, with time, the two methods settled down happily side by side, and in the growing complex of the firm's workshops today there can now be found not only the machines with their operators but workers in a score or so of other crafts, all playing their part in feeding the lavish window and show-case displays 'in front': smelters, beaters, chisellers, engravers, planishers, burnishers, gem-setters, enamellers.

The firm was first known as Louis Wolfers Père et Fils, and was solely a wholesale producer. When in 1890 its first retail shop was opened, old Louis Wolfers retired, refusing to become 'a shopkeeper'. Later the name was changed successively to Wolfers Frères and then to Wolfers Frères, S.A.

Railway development in Brussels caused the demolition of the old workshops and of the retail store, the place of both

being taken by the present fine buildings, specially erected, in
rue d'Arenberg. In turn even these became too cramped, and
are still being enlarged as opportunity offers. The third and
fourth generation of this illustrious dynasty are now at the head
of affairs, and their work, in gold, ivory, precious woods,
marbles, lacquers and gems, appears in museums all over Europe,
and even in the New World. The firm was the first Belgian
enterprise to overstep the frontiers and make a name for itself
at international exhibitions.

For long it refused to concern itself, in the matter of jewellery
and table-ware, with any other metals but gold, platinum and
silver. With changing social conditions, however, there arose
the problem of providing full employment in working these,
and the firm began to produce high-grade silver plate side by
side with the purer metals. Powerful hydraulic presses of 800 and
1,000 tons can be seen making this silver plate.

'Wolfers' which is as affectionately known all over Belgium
and beyond as its familiar trade mark of the 'W' and boar's head,
spans a long period of social change. The first piece of silver
plating was achieved by electro-chemistry in 1840, and less than
ten years after that Louis Wolfers was producing the first silver
spoons and forks by machinery. At that time only the rich owned
silver; the spoons and forks of the ordinary man were of wood
and pewter. It was the speedier production of Louis Wolfers
which led to one great change among the well-to-do: instead
of his own personal table-set being brought along for use by each
visitor invited to a meal, the householder was able to acquire
enough silver-ware to have the table laid for his guests.

As a sample of the kind of task Wolfers takes in its stride two
commissions of the present century may be quoted. The great
medieval Cloth Hall of Ypres, one of the architectural glories of
western Flanders, was destroyed by bombardment during the
first world war. When it was rebuilt the King and Queen of
England attended its reopening. A yard-long model of the hall

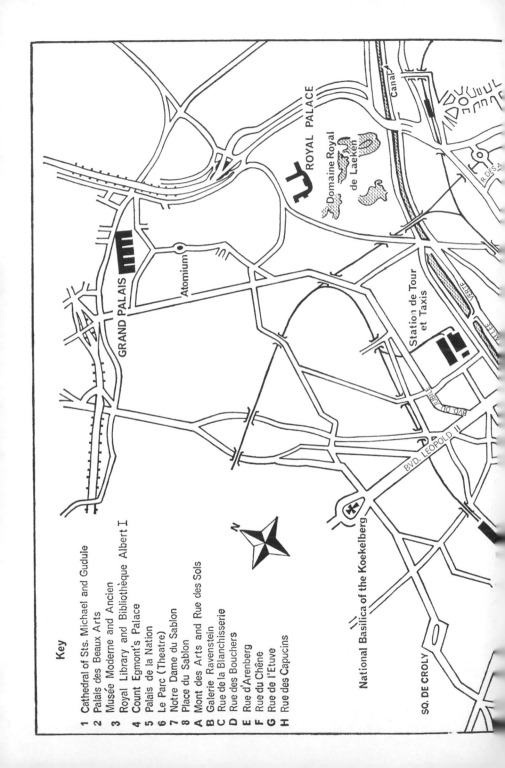

Key

1 Cathedral of Sts. Michael and Gudule
2 Palais des Beaux Arts
3 Musée Moderne and Ancien
4 Royal Library and Bibliothèque Albert I
4 Count Egmont's Palace
5 Palais de la Nation
6 Le Parc (Theatre)
7 Notre Dame du Sablon
8 Place du Sablon
A Mont des Arts and Rue des Sols
B Galerie Ravenstein
C Rue de la Blanchisserie
D Rue des Bouchers
E Rue d'Arenberg
F Rue du Chêne
G Rue de l'Etuve
H Rue des Capucins

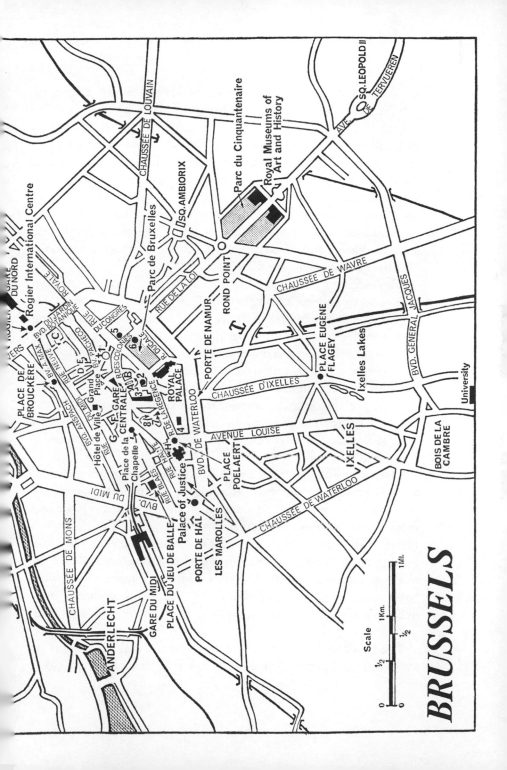

BRUSSELS

SQ. LEOPOLD II

AVE. DE TERVUEREN

CHAUSSÉE DE LOUVAIN

SQ. AMBIORIX

Parc de Bruxelles

Parc du Cinquantenaire

Royal Museums of Art and History

RUE DE LA LOI

RUE DU CONGRÈS

ROND POINT

CHAUSSÉE DE WAVRE

Rogier International Centre

GARE DU NORD

BVD. DU JARDIN BOTANIQUE

RUE ROYALE

BV. A. MAX.

RUE NEUVE

BVD. ANSPACH

BV. PACHECO

RUE DESCOLONIES

PLACE DE BROUCKÈRE

Hôtel de Ville

Grand Place

Place de la CENTRALE

GARE

RUE DUCALE

ROYAL PALACE

PORTE DE NAMUR

PLACE EUGÈNE FLAGEY

Ixelles Lakes

BVD. GÉNÉRAL JACQUES

CHAUSSÉE D'IXELLES

Chapelle

RUE HTE.

RUE DE LA RÉGENCE

RUE BLAES

RUE HTE.

DU MIDI

BVD.

Palace of Justice

PORTE DE HAL

LES MAROLLES

PLACE DU JEU DE BALLE

CHAUSSÉE DE MONS

GARE DU MIDI

ANDERLECHT

BVD. DE WATERLOO

PLACE POELAERT

AVENUE LOUISE

IXELLES

CHAUSSÉE DE WATERLOO

BOIS DE LA CAMBRE

University

Scale

½   0   1Km.   1Ml.

½

in solid silver, with the hundreds of statues which appear on the original reproduced in gold, was made by the firm for presentation to Their Majesties on behalf of the thousands of Belgians who had been refugees in England during the war.

As an expression of admiration and gratitude for the achievements of the American forces in the campaigns in and around Bastogne, in south-eastern Belgium, the Belgian ambassador to the United States presented President Truman with a casket made in malachite, silver and precious woods, containing earth collected in the copses of Bastogne. It bears the proud inscription: 'Wolfers Frères *fecit*: 1947.'

This account of a grand tradition which nurtures its own loyalties can end with a slight but charming story. Recently De Coster, the senior master-chiseller, rose to his feet one morning as the manager passed through the workshops. With a bow he uttered the time-honoured formula of the gild-member who feels the time has come for retirement: 'Monsieur, je vous remets mon marteau.' The hammer which he handed back is one of the treasures of the firm; its once-sturdy wooden handle is, in the middle, where this craftsman's thumb and forefinger pressed against it daily for sixty-one years, worn down to the thinness of a biscuit.

Many who know little else about Brussels can murmur mechanically: 'Brussels for carpets.' A pleasure more deeply satisfying than watching any rapid production on power looms is to be had from a visit to Etablissements Chaudoir, in the rue des Aîles. Here, in another family business, can be seen the designing and making of tapestries by hand, just as in medieval times. Less than thirty women are employed, each working at a pedal frame, with hand-dyed, moth-proofed wools of delightful colours, rich, delicate and sombre, upon designs evolved within the same four walls.

The tapestries are of widely differing sizes, and the designs of every style and period. Some bring to life a scene of bygone days;

Shellfish are very popular,
especially mussels (*page 16*)

The great tower of the Church of La Chapelle

Looming over every narrow alley of Les Marolles is the Palais de Justice (*page 19*)

The new extension of
Saint Peter's Hospital, for
centuries a *léproserie*,
swept away part of Les
Marolles (*page 20*)

Students at Brussels Uni-
versity, which has no
religious bias

◁ . . . old locks,
keys of every
kind . . . ' (*page*
2)

A medieval- ▷
style tapestry
made in a world-
famous family
workshop of
today (*page 40*)

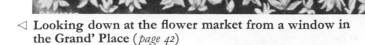

◁ Looking down at the flower market from a window in
the Grand' Place (*page 42*)

The Atomium, its polished spheres pricked with
innumerable flickering coloured lights, is brilliant
by night (*page 44*)
◁

the bric-à-brac stalls.
A bargain is still
possible ' (*page 23*)

Erasmus's stud is kept as it wa four hundred years ago (page 62)

The vast International Rogier Centre, which offers facilities to business men from all over the world (*page 72*)

The boulevard Adolphe Max at night

'It is worth pausing to watch the traffic policeman on duty in the place de Brouckère'. Note Rodin's sculptures on the Bourse (*page 78*)

others are studies of sunshine on flowers, of autumn woods, of
stylized birds in formal gardens. Here may be a colossal dandelion-
clock, worked in greys and silvers, casting abroad its seeds
against floating clouds and blue sky; over there are abstract
patterns which are merely an expression of the designer's delight
in playing with colours and shapes.

But do not, whatever you do, miss a wonderful piece in
medieval style which hangs in the wide front hall of the present
ruler of this kingdom, Mme Dambiermont-Chaudoir. It shows
a hunting scene in a dark and mysterious forest; tall trees with
straight trunks and the much-too-large leaves always seen in
work of the period form a frieze in the background; the green
floor of the wood is starred with harebells, campion and violets.
Three huntsmen with golden, shoulder-length hair and wearing
the dress of the Middle Ages, mounted on richly harnessed horses
and aided by one white hound, are pursuing a stag, and blowing
tall, curving, brass horns. There is a placid other-worldliness
about the look of all the participants in this moment, frozen and
preserved from another age. Even the stag, gracefully rearing
upon its hind legs as the horses are, seems more concerned with
keeping its place in a lovely pattern of movement than in escaping
from the equally dreamlike hound and horsemen.

Etablissements Chaudoir have a worldwide renown. When I
was last there two priceless tapestries, one from a museum in
London and the other from one in New York, were stretched
upon neighbouring hand-frames for repairs. And anyone wonder-
ing if these patient women loved their work would gain an
instant answer from the impossibility of knowing, even with
their help, where was the ancient work, and where the new and
healing stitchery of the twentieth century.

D

Chapter 7

Out and About

BRUSSELS provides a rich assortment of outdoor trips, long and short. Even on foot, many a pleasant morning or afternoon excursion can be made, and by the use of the Tram Vicinale (local tramcar service) it is possible to go as far as twelve miles outside the city into the green belt around it.

Everyone visiting Brussels makes for the Grand' Place soon after arrival, either on the first evening, to admire the flood-lighting, or next day to see what is really the heart of Brussels in every sense of that overworked word. But many people miss, simply because they do not know about it, one of the most delightful aspects of the Grand' Place: its use in the very early hours of the morning for the purpose for which it was intended—a market.

Here, from just before dawn onwards, the wholesale dealers in vegetables and *salades*, pot-plants and fruit, take their stand. The bustle, clatter and litter are indescribable, but what is equally worth seeing is the vigour and completeness with which every last cabbage-stalk and lettuce-leaf is tidied away and the great square hosed and swept in readiness for the day's business in the City Hall and other surrounding buildings, which begins at about nine o'clock.

For the rest of the day, though, a good-sized area in the middle of the square is allowed to be used as a retail market for bedding plants and cut flowers. And a flower market in any part of Belgium, a country of flower-lovers, is always a fine sight, especially from overhead. If you are on the upper floors of the museum in the King's House opposite the City Hall, be sure to look out of a window, whatever the time of day, for spread below there will be a 'Brussels carpet' indeed, of a brilliance and magnificence to make you cry out.

On Sunday mornings the square is used as a bird market, and some may enjoy this but others find it saddening. Another market, of more universal interest, also held on Sunday mornings, is the antiques market of the traders with premises around the Place du Sablon. There everything is a very good example of its kind, even though offered for sale on street stalls with brilliant awnings.

The first thing that strikes anyone going into the streets of Brussels is the material used in their surfacing. The thrifty burghers of the past saw to it that they were laid with cobbles, and these have lasted so long that it is possible to recognize the many streets created in the last hundred years by the fact that they are not cobbled. Holiday-makers in Brussels who have come unprepared for cobbles, and unsuitably shod, soon find out how painful they can be to walk on.

The stranger will also notice the immense amount of street trading which goes on in the old town, both on barrows for the sale of newspapers, fruit, flowers and sweets, shellfish and *frites*, and at canopied stalls for tobacco and cigarettes, small souvenirs, postcards, magazines, ball-pens and the like. There are other stalls for the sale of tickets for the national lotteries, and 'blind' kiosks on almost every pavement corner. These are stout round pillars with a 'coolie-hat' capping, the effect of the whole being rather like a pepper-pot, and are used for advertising by means of sticker-posters such things as performances at theatres, night clubs and circuses, or illumination displays in public parks. Trade and commercial advertisements do not appear on them.

The trams of Brussels are also a familiar feature: long, single-decked vehicles, cream-coloured, with a standing platform at the rear where the passengers enter, and a double-door exit half

way along one side. On the city routes tickets can be had which
will cover up to a dozen journeys on any route the passenger
likes to select, with spaces for punching by the conductor. The
trams on the city routes are numbered, and the long-distance
Vicinales are lettered. Traffic keeps to the right, as in all continental countries except Sweden.

An expedition which most people are tempted to make is to
the Atomium, which can be seen from the windows of high
buildings all over Brussels and from street level in many parts
of the upper town. Like the Eiffel Tower of Paris, it was originally
built mainly as an 'attraction gimmick' for an exhibition, in
this case the Universal and International Exhibition of 1958.
Centre of the exhibition and focus of all eyes in the grounds and
for a long distance in and outside Brussels, the towering and
glittering Atomium is a model of a molecule in the crystal state.
When the exhibition closed, this was left as the great year of 1958
had seen it. It consists of eight spheres, made of light metal alloy,
arranged so as to form the eight corners of a cube, with a ninth
to mark its centre. This central sphere is joined to all the others,
and the others joined each to the next, by a series of metal tubes
ten feet in diameter, containing escalators and staircases, so that
all the fifty-nine-foot globes can be entered. The whole is no
less than three hundred and forty feet high, so placed that it
appears to be poised on a sphere forming one of the corners of
the cube, and it shines in the sunlight like the purest silver.

All nine globes are covered with innumerable 'portholes',
each just large enough to take an electric-light bulb. These bulbs
are of many colours, and they all flicker on and off rapidly after
dark; with the reflection of all other light on the polished spheres
the effect is most brilliant.

A lift runs directly from the lowest globe to the highest,
climbing the distance in twenty seconds, and in this top globe
is a restaurant capable of seating a hundred and forty people,
with tremendous views from its girdle of large windows, but as

may be imagined it is by no means a cheap place at which to eat. The other spheres, connected for ascent by escalators, and for descent by staircases, contain scientific displays illustrating the peaceful uses of atomic energy.

While in the neighbourhood of the exhibition grounds it is easy to visit the country home of the Belgian royal family at Laeken. The palace gardens are open to the public, and the greenhouses also on certain days in the late spring. Here, as at the royal palace in the city, the khaki-clad, white-belted sentries, motionless in their red-yellow-and-black striped boxes, are a feature of the scene. More noticeable still, in the Laeken grounds, are the fantastic Japanese Tower and Chinese Pavilion. These were bought by King Leopold II after the Paris Exhibition of 1900. I do not think that you will very much admire Notre-Dame de Laeken, the royal church in Laeken village, with its extraordinary mixture of styles and its over-elaborated decoration.

If you are taking a holiday in Brussels in the very late summer you are almost certain to be there at the time of one or other of the many *braderies* which take place at intervals all through the autumn. These are shopping festivals, confined to one or two streets, and run as a community effort. There is elaborate decoration, with many fairy-lights and much noisy music, and manifold 'special offers' aimed at catching custom; some very staggering window displays accompany them. It is worth while to ask at the City Hall for information about possible *braderies*, as there is something delightfully reminiscent of a country village about the friendly and very 'localized' atmosphere of these efforts. Even if no *braderie* offers itself for your amusement, you are extremely likely to run into a fair, for of these there are literally scores in Brussels alone, in the course of a year; almost any unimportant public square, or even a bomb-site, will serve to accommodate one. The citizens adore them, and their pleasure is a joy to watch.

When you are out on the fringe of Brussels for any purpose you cannot fail to notice something very odd: market gardens, spreading over vast areas and consisting solely of long, raked-up mounds of earth, like endless graves, with at one end a building like a hen-house having a stumpy metal chimney upon its roof. These are the culture grounds for chicory, known in Brussels as *witloof* (whiteleaf), a popular vegetable, and under the beds of light, sandy earth run hot pipes to encourage its growth.

On the western edge of Brussels, coming close up to the city's first buildings, are fields of hops. But the most interesting of the near-home crops of Brussels is the enormous black table-grape, grown in large quantities in the Hoeilaart district, on the eastern fringe. Here is a city of low-pitched greenhouses, which boasts that it can produce on any day of the year bunches of grapes which have just then reached their peak of perfection. There is even a Grape Fair here in September each year.

Within easy reach of the city by Tram Vicinale, for these cover nearly the whole of the province of Brabant, are three interesting châteaux: one empty, but restored from its former ruin; one converted into an hotel (this sounds dull, but it isn't), and one preserved in every detail as it was when last lived in, and now open as a museum and gallery of art.

The first of these, Beersel, is like something straight out of a fairy-story. Rounding a bend in a country lane, you come suddenly upon it, forming an island near one shore of a tree-girt lakelet, and linked to the bank by a footbridge. This is now a permanent structure, but was formerly built in such a way as to be easily dismantled in the event of an attack.

The mass of the castle, part of the ancient south-western defences of Brussels, frowns across the still, leaf-starred water. It has three towers, round on the side towards the lake, but flat where they face inward on to the castle courtyard. They are joined by the loopholed curtain-wall which bounds the island and are themselves pierced by look-out windows and slots for crossbows. The windows on the flat, inner side of each tower are much larger, having been planned to light the rooms. The torture chamber, complete with all its evil appurtenances, can be seen inside the castle.

Beersel was built in the thirteenth century and lived in by the Witthem family for more than four hundred years. Later it passed by marriage to two other families, and then, early in the last century, became a cotton-mill. That did not last long, and it was allowed to fall into ruin, till finally it was given by the owners of the land on which it is built to a society known as the Friends of the Château of Beersel. By them it was restored, to become the fascinating place of excursion into the Middle Ages which it is today.

Folklore and historical plays, including Shakespeare, are performed in the castle courtyard during the summer months. The floodlit towers and ramparts form a backcloth finer than any dramatist could dream of.

Where the footbridge reaches the lake shore there is an inn with an interior strikingly like an illustration one might imagine for the stories of the Brothers Grimm, or those seen on the canvases of the Flemish painter Breughel. It is all, however, an ingenious trick; though very ancient bricks, beams, floor-pavings, staircase and even window-glass were used, and the furnishings carefully chosen from antique sources to match, the Auberge des Chevaliers dates only from 1933.

Gaesbeek, which is much larger, and has always been quite complete, is not far off. This was built a hundred years after Beersel, and has never stood uninhabited. Its last private owner was an Italian lady, the Marchesa d'Arconati-Visconti, who made it over with all its contents to the Belgian nation in 1921. It remains just as she left it, and holds a wealth of lovely things: carvings in wood, ivory and alabaster; fine furniture, paintings, tapestries and carpets. Marchesa Visconti must have been thinking tenderly of these last when she stipulated, as a condition of her gift, that a charge be made for admission so that 'the carpets should not be soiled by the multitudes'. Breughel was very

often at Gaesbeek, and he sometimes painted from the courtyard and windows, which explains why so many of the views
seem to be familiar.

One delightful feature of Gaesbeek is the complete surprise
of coming out of doors into its Italian garden, which on the
château side follows the semicircle of the house itself. From the
outside the building appears forbidding, having very few windows on its outer façade, but it has a gracious and friendly frontage on to the garden, which is laid out in what was formerly the
courtyard of the fortress. The whole is again an island, only here
the moat is almost dry.

Huizingen is like a pocket-sized Versailles, and is set on the
edge of a large lake with swans. There is an extensive and lovely
domain with statuary, where tennis, mini-golf, archery, boating
on the lake and other sports can be enjoyed by the public, since
the whole place is now the property of the province of Brabant.
There is also a fine swimming-pool and the greenhouses are open
daily. The house itself is an hotel and restaurant, but two of the
most delightful features of the whole are the displays of rare
flowering plants and the fact that the place is a bird reserve. It is
a very popular spot with Brussels people on Saturday and Sunday
afternoons, and its peace and attraction for the visitor from abroad
can better be appreciated on other days.

West of Brussels, in a village named Hekelghem, is a vogue
for a curious local art: *Zandtapijten*, or sand carpets. Several of
the cafés have these; they are to be found in a ground-floor room
or rooms, where the floors have been rebuilt so as to provide a
slight ramp, sloping upwards from the door. Visitors are penned
behind a barrier, and on the ramp are found copies of famous
(and not-so-famous) paintings, executed in coloured sands laid
down on the planking. Occasionally one whole room will be
taken up by one picture, if the work to be reproduced is a very
large one, as for example Peter Paul Rubens's 'Descent from the
Cross', or Rembrandt's 'Night Watch'. The copy of the picture,

considering the material used, is surprisingly good, even if the colouring is rather harsh.

Many visitors to Brussels travel out to Waterloo. Here is the site of a battle which, though it was fought more than a century and a half ago, still captures the interest of most people. Waterloo lies twelve miles south of Brussels on the 'W' route of the Tram Vicinale. The country around is not beautiful, but one can visit the posting inn, in the main street of the village. This was used by Wellington as his headquarters, and here he wrote his historic dispatch announcing the victory, which incidentally gave to the battle the name it has ever since borne. In the inn, quaintly known as Au Quartier Général de Wellington, are preserved a number of his personal belongings and the furniture he used. In a garden to the right of the church is a most unusual monument, marking the spot at which Lord Uxbridge chose to have his leg buried— as near as possible, it is said, to the churchyard—after it had been shot off in the battle.

The outstanding feature of the village is the great Lion of Waterloo. This, cast from captured French cannon, is set on a high mound of earth, with steps to its summit, and faces towards France, as if still defending Brussels from the invader. The mound —the largest artificial mound in Europe—was piled by local labour as a tribute to the victorious forces.

There is also an interesting three-dimensional panorama, which represents the whole field of battle as it would have been seen from where the Lion now stands, and in a building across the road a film is shown which reconstructs the course of the battle.

If the country round Waterloo is disappointing, the visitor is more than compensated by the early part of the journey from Brussels to the village, which takes him through what is really a portion of the vast and splendid Forêt de Soignes. This is to Brussels what the Bois de Boulogne is to Paris, and is a surviving part of the primeval forest which once covered most of ancient Gaul.

Imagine a performing seal in profile before you, facing to your left, with a beach ball balanced on its nose, and you have the relative outlines of the Forêt and of Brussels itself, the seal being the great forest and the circle of the ball the city of Brussels. Thus closely, indeed, do the trees approach the urban area, running in some places right up to the garden walls of the large houses which fill that quarter.

As late as 1822 there were still thirty thousand acres of it. But building enterprise was shrinking it with disquieting rapidity, and Leopold I finally succeeded in persuading his government to buy what was left for the nation: even then— and remaining that much today—a lordly eleven thousand acres.

Nowhere else in Europe is there as large a forest area with such unity of tree species; it is almost entirely beech. At all seasons of the year this forest is lovely. The great silver-green trunks rise like the close-set pillars of a vast cathedral and the leafy branches burst into sun-shot fountains against the blue air, and that is spring. Or there may be a carpet of white silence, with the leafless twigs an iron filigree against a greyer sky, and a fiery sunset blazing behind it all, and that is winter. When all the golden coins stored in all the treasure-chests of the world have been scattered at your feet, it is autumn.

Here are ravines with chuckling brooks, and the shade-spattered forest floor as it has been for centuries. And if the visitor can be quiet enough, and ready to freeze in an instant to a pillar of entranced watching, he may glimpse for a few breathless moments a gentle-eyed hind or a russet-coated roe-buck, before it glides with the silence of a shadow between the beech trunks, and is gone.

Chapter 8

'To Stand and Stare'

BRUSSELS is a wonderful city in which 'to stand and stare', and even those who declare that they do not enjoy museums find here such a wide choice of interests and the displays so cleverly arranged that they are inclined to forget that what they are looking at is a museum at all, and indeed it is not, in the usual sense of the word.

One of the most fascinating of these places has also the merit of being very easy to find: it is the House of the Brewers, one of the thirty-three matchless houses on the Grand' Place. It is not at all difficult to pick out this house from the rest, though at first glance all seem so much alike, since it stands among the group of five which are on the same side of the Place as the City Hall, and has on the apex of its gable the equestrian statue of Charles of Lorraine. Moreover, amongst the gilded decorations on its façade is the inscription 'Maison des Brasseurs'.

The house has a fine interior, with broad, oak-panelled corridors and tiled or parquet floors, polished with typically Flemish pride. The visitor is shown the handsome Salle de Conseil, where meetings of the various Gilds of Brewers are held. Each stained-glass window here shows the crest of a different brewers' association.

The implement most used by a brewer is the wooden *fourquet*, or malt-shovel: an oval 'spade' with a handle six or seven feet long, its scoop pierced by several longitudinal slits. With this the malt is stirred and partially strained in the brewing-vats. The Fraternity of Master-Brewers is known as the Chevaliers du

Fourquet—the Knights of the Malt-Shovel—and everywhere in this lovely old gild house examples of antique *fourquets* are to be seen, hanging up or leaning against the walls.

The Master-Brewers, the aristocracy of the Belgian brewing trade, also meet in the Maison des Brasseurs but have their own council hall, distinct from the meeting-place used by the individual gilds. This is not, and does not need to be, capable of holding anything like so large a company, but it is a very beautiful room, again lighted by stained-glass windows, and has three splendid brazen chandeliers hanging by chains from the ceiling, which still use their dozens of hand-dipped, golden tallow candles.

But the pride of the house is in the basement, where the completely equipped medieval brewing-cellar can be seen, with its vast wooden vats, malt-shovels, pan-strainers, ladles and skimmers. Part of this great room was a cooperage, and this also is in its original state, with the tools, wood and partly completed barrels lying about.

Adjoining it is a complete—though in this case still functioning —medieval tavern, with stone-slabbed floor, rough walls of ancient brick, long low stained-glass windows at pavement level, simply carpentered tables, benches and stools, shiny from constant use, and a fine stone-arched fireplace with huge logs piled in the iron basket. Here are served the products of Belgium's greatest brewing firms, and as the place seems to be used mainly by those visiting the Maison des Brasseurs for sightseeing, it is calm and uncrowded. Here in accurate detail is the background against which the characters of many a Breughel painting drank their beer, told their rough jokes and laughed their hearty laughter.

Across the Grand' Place from the Brewers' headquarters is the Maison du Roi, and this houses the Musée Communal of Brussels; the collections here shown form in themselves an abridged history of the city's sometimes stormy and always interesting past.

This handsome building, if not as beautiful as the Hôtel de Ville opposite, has a distinguished exterior, fully in keeping with the rest of the Grand' Place. Its original name was The Bread House, and it is supposed that here the Gild of Bakers had their headquarters. Later it became a kind of rating office for the province of Brabant. Then at the beginning of the sixteenth century the Emperor Charles V had it completely rebuilt, giving it the external aspect it has today. It received its title of Maison du Roi in reference to the King of Spain. Still later it was private property for a time, but the city acquired it again in 1860, reconstructed its interior and housed its fine collections there. These tell the story of Brussels from many points of view, assisting the student of civic life, politics, handcrafts, architecture and trade.

The museum as such owes its existence to an English resident, John Waterloo Wilson, who offered to the city in 1878 his collection of twenty-six Flemish, French and Dutch pictures, which at that time were on exhibition in the Fine Arts Academy in Brussels. Three years later he bequeathed a substantial sum to the municipality for the purchase of additional works of art.

It would take more than a book of this size to list everything that the visitor should see in the Maison du Roi, but a few things must be spoken of here. Of prime importance, even to the ordinary visitor with an unspecialized interest, are two magnificent carved and painted altar-pieces illustrating the life of the Blessed Virgin Mary, made in Brussels, the one at the end of the fifteenth and the other early in the sixteenth century. There are also eight statues of prophets, dating from about 1380, removed from the porch of the old Hôtel de Ville, and numerous paintings, engravings and old street maps telling the story of the city's architectural past. One very fine anonymous picture shows many different kinds of artisans—stonemasons, sculptors, slaters and so on—at their work, so that it can be seen exactly what kinds of tools they used.

There is also a large collection of objects relating to bygone trade gilds—weights, measures, document chests and the like—and one room is given up to coins, medals and seals of the past. The Lace Room is a step into fairyland; most visitors who see the fine old pieces on display find it hard to believe that human hands have fashioned anything so gossamer-frail.

Brussels has always been famed for its pottery and porcelain, and all this is finely represented here. Another room of great interest is that illustrating the revolution of July 1830 which gave Belgium its independence. Down through its long history the country has been under various rulers: Burgundy, Spain, Austria, France and, last of them all, Holland. After the Napoleonic Wars the Congress of Vienna nominated Prince William of Orange-Nassau to be ruler of a combined kingdom, which was to be called 'Holland and Belgium'. Holland being Protestant and Belgium Catholic, this turned out a very unhappy arrangement, and there was a period of nothing better than sullen acceptance on both sides of a state of affairs desired by neither. Belgium, and of course Brussels, enjoyed no free press and no freedom for Catholic education.

In 1830 underground resentments exploded within the city itself; the province of Brabant quickly followed into the revolt and free Belgium was born. It chose a constitutional monarchy, and offered the crown to Prince Leopold of Saxe Coburg-Gotha on 21st July 1831, amid great rejoicing.

Flags and weapons used in the rebellion are in the section named 'Libre Belgique' at the King's House; also decrees, orders to troops and pamphlets addressed to the people; pictures showing some of the fighting in the streets and other events, and the original manuscript and score of the national anthem of the new Belgium: *La Brabançonne*.

The Wilson Room contains the collection which formed the nucleus of the Musée Communal, and a nineteenth-century room traces by means of pictures the rapid architectural development of the city since 1830. Leopold II was a great planner and builder, and set himself industriously to the project of dignifying his capital. He it was who in 1871 had the River Senne, in many places no more than an unlovely and unsavoury ditch, vaulted over, and set up above it so many of the fine buildings of today: the Bourse, the Royal Museum, the Palace of Justice. He also planned the cutting of the highways linking the city with Boits-fort, Laeken and Tervueren, and the laying out of the parks of Woluwe, Forest, Schaerbeek and Laeken.

One of the exhibits in the Maison du Roi which scarcely a single visitor fails to seek out is the Wardrobe Room of Man-neken-Pis, a large apartment on the second floor. It contains the most remarkable collection of miniature clothing in the world. Regiments, municipalities, gilds and individual donors vie with one another in increasing the range of the Manneken's wardrobe. At the time I last saw his 'Précieux Vestiaire' he possessed no less than a hundred and sixty-nine outfits, and this total is ever on the increase.

Each costume is presented to the Manneken with due ceremony. He is arrayed in the new suit in the morning, and then veiled by some flag appropriate to the nationality of the donor. Later in the day, in the presence of the Burgomaster, the gift is formally handed over by the unveiling of the statue, before the outfit goes across the Grand' Place to join the other exhibits in the Wardrobe Room. Many of the dresses are of great value, decked in hand embroideries, gold lace, brass buttons, satin facings, feathers and fringes, in exact imitation of their originals, and each is exhibited on a plaster facsimile of the Manneken himself, so that it can be seen exactly how he looks wearing it.

All kinds of national and peasant costumes are included, and many trades and callings; he can be a miner of southern Belgium, complete with pick and lamp, a Congolese warrior, a lawyer of the Brussels Court of Appeal, a Basque *souletin* (dancer), an American Indian in full war-paint, a Chinese mandarin, a United

States marine. He possesses the uniforms of several schools and the outfits of a number of famous sports teams, which of course demand a football, canoe, bicycle or even crossbow. The testimonials, 'loyal addresses' and diplomas which have been offered to him by colleges and learned societies all over the world are also on show.

In the minds of most people Brussels as a museum centre means chiefly Flemish art, and it is to the Musée Ancien that everyone goes who wants to see Netherlands painting at its best. Here are the lovely grave Madonnas of Rogier van der Weyden, Hugo van der Goes, Memling, van Eyck and Mabuse; the sumptuous portraiture of Rubens; the restrained elegance of Vandyck; the earthy, vulgar enjoyment of carousing peasantry and the familiar Brabantine landscape of the canvases of Pieter Breughel the Elder; the smooth, glowing Dutch interiors, flavoured strongly with a kind of self-satisfied yet entirely justifiable pride in good furniture and appointments which is so faithfully noted down by Pieter de Hooch and Gabriel Metsu.

As you go about Brussels outside this museum, keep your eyes open. In the windows of antique shops, in the parlours behind humble shops of many another kind, glimpsed through their briefly opened doors as the proprietor's wife bustles through to serve you, you will see the tall polished cupboards, the high-backed chairs, the long windows, the shining brass, the spotless tiled floors that you saw in many of these paintings. More fascinatingly still, the same faces will pass you in the streets; you will see the grave, gentle Madonna, the shyly smiling waitress who brought to a guest a glass of wine in some painted court-yard, the rosy-cheeked village boy, the unshaven farm worker. Some of the pleasure of a walk in the streets of Brussels lies in finding these pictured figures, immortalized for centuries on the canvases of the painters, still going about their daily business before your eyes, their very expressions unchanged.

But this gallery does not lack the work of painters of other races. Italians like Tiepolo, Tintoretto and Crivelli, and French masters such as Boucher, Fragonard and Lorraine are here too. The Musée Moderne, quite near, carries the works of many fine European painters of the last hundred years; these names are possibly less well known to the visitor. At the Cinquantenaire Arch are the Royal Museums of Art and History, holding collections of Assyrian, Greek, Egyptian and Roman antiquities mainly of interest to the specialist scholar.

There is a treat for the lover of dainty medieval miniatures in the manuscript section of the Royal Library. Here may be seen pages of vellum bearing exquisitely illuminated French, German, Spanish, English and Italian texts of gospels and books of prayers of the eighth to the sixteenth centuries. In pictures sometimes no larger than a postage stamp, their colours glowing as if applied last week, are gems of scriptural scenes: Adam and Eve in Eden, the Tree of Jesse, the Nativity of Jesus, the Calling of the Apostles, carried out with a loving devotion to the incredibly close detail demanded that is nothing short of miraculous. Around the edges of the pages ramble enchanting decorated borders, with flowers, butterflies, birds, insects, stars, bunches of grapes, corn and everything that the imagination of the scribe could devise to add to the glory of his work.

This collection, and the wealth of other book and manuscript treasures preserved in this library, have a fame so worldwide that something should be said here of its past and of the remarkable possibilities of its future. Its history is bound up with that of the Belgian people from long before they bore that name, for in the fifteenth century the territory formed a part of the immensely wealthy dukedom of Burgundy. These Burgundian dukes, wise and knowledgeable patrons of the arts, amassed a fine collection of illuminated manuscripts in their various residences in the Low Countries, a collection which became a legend even in their own time. It was Philip II, during the sovereignty of Spain, who converted this Burgundian Collection, as it is still known, into a

E

Royal Library in 1559, by causing it to be assembled in the Coudenberg Palace in Brussels. An inventory taken by its first librarian gives a total of nine hundred and sixty works.

The Manuscript Room of the present Royal Library still houses the Burgundian Collection, though all the collections are due to be removed to the new Albertine building on the Mont des Arts, which at the time of writing is practically ready to receive them. Many of the manuscript treasures are of world renown, as for example the *Chroniques de Hainaut*, comprising forty miniatures in the purest style of the Flemish school, and the *Breviary of Philip the Good*, another marvel of illumination executed in Flanders early in the second half of the fifteenth century. The *Conquêtes de Charlemagne* provides a wonderful series of *grisaille* miniatures, this type of work being an outstanding characteristic of Flemish books.

The Burgundian sovereigns combined a catholic taste with vast wealth, and accordingly there are also many foreign manuscripts of incalculable value. Among these pride of place is held by the *Belles Heures* of the Duc de Berry.

In 1511 Margaret of Austria, Regent of the Low Countries, had acquired the library of Prince Charles de Croy, and this she bequeathed to a niece who later left it to Philip II. This was the first of four centuries of additions to the library which have continued ever since, and it was described by a contemporary document as consisting of 'lxxviii volumes writ fair by hand on parchment'.

The religious wars of the sixteenth century brought about a long period of neglect of the library, and it was not until the reign of Maria Theresa of Austria that anything more was done for it. The Empress appointed Count Cobenzl as her minister plenipotentiary and on arrival in Brussels he was horrified to find priceless treasures mouldering on the shelves and 'the wildest disorder everywhere'. He took drastic action at once, and nominated a librarian who drew up an adequate catalogue and threw the library open to the public. By the end of the eighteenth century the collections had increased enormously, a leading example of acquisitions at that time being the manuscript of Thomas à Kempis's *Imitation of Christ*.

At the time of the French Revolution there was wholesale pillage of the library, when occupying French forces removed 'seven long carts' of manuscripts and books to Paris. These, however, were ordered to be returned after the defeat of Napoleon, to the number, says a contemporary writer, of 929 printed books and 621 manuscripts. By 1827 the total number of works was 2,900, and ever since then the collections have steadily been increased.

A few figures will give some idea of the responsibilities of the chief librarian of the present day:

Printed Works Department	2,000,000 volumes
Rare Books Section	33,000 volumes
Maps and Charts Division	35,000 exhibits
Manuscript Room	34,000 exhibits
Department of Coins and Medals	250,000 pieces
Print Room	650,000 documents

This last includes two remarkable series of engravings by Breughel and Rubens.

It is only natural that in the course of years the Royal Library should have several times outgrown its accommodation. Since the death of Albert I of Belgium in 1934 there has been a movement to provide it with a really adequate home. The highly up-to-date Bibliothèque Albert Iᵉʳ, erected in his memory, has seventeen storeys and over five hundred windows in one façade alone. It will ultimately provide some seventy-two miles of shelving, as against eighteen miles in the old building, and a pneumatic conveyor system already ensures that any book requested, regardless of the floor from which it may come, can be in the hands of its borrower within six minutes. The Bibliothèque de Bourgogne, by the time these words are read, will be

occupying an air-conditioned strong room in the remotest part
of what Brussels itself describes as 'this incomparable centre of
intellect'.

The library publishes a loose-leaf portfolio of forty-eight re-
productions in full colour of the loveliest of the miniatures in the
Manuscript Room, and though this, as may well be imagined, is
by no means cheap, it is one of the most lasting and satisfying
souvenirs of a visit to Brussels which can be found anywhere.

In the rue de la Régence, about midway between the Palais de
Justice and the home of the Belgian royal family, is another
museum, considered to be the richest and most important of its
kind in the world, although it is comparatively limited in size.
This is the Museum of Musical Instruments of the Brussels
Conservatoire of Music. Here in twenty-eight rooms are four
thousand instruments from every country and of all periods, of
which a hundred and fifty have no known duplicate example.
Their very names are music in themselves: harpsichords, virginals,
spinets, bass viols, lutes, dulcimers, theorbos, chitaroni. Here
too are strange instruments from the East, the Pacific and Africa,
such as the *tayuc* (peacock) from India. A miniature piano played
on by Mozart when a child has a proud place, and many of the
larger keyboard instruments are beautifully decorated with inlay
or paintings.

The Musée du Dynastie (the 'Royal Family Museum'), quite
near to the Royal Palace, is of fascinating interest, especially the
everyday personal possessions of the five Belgian monarchs to
date: toys, books, clothing, jewellery, letters, pictures. An
attractive notion for a spare hour is to visit the porte de Hal, on
the Inner Ring Road, the only one of the ancient gates of Brussels
still standing. This is now isolated in the midst of the boulevard's
stream of traffic, and has become a museum of ancient weapons,
some terrifying, some amusing.

At Tervueren, a north-east suburb, is the world-renowned
Congo Museum, and within Brussels itself the Charlier House in

rue du Dynastie merits a visit too. This is the home of a former aristocratic family of Brussels; fitted up entirely with the kind of lovely furniture and appointments which would be used by a household of this standing, it provides a real feast of bygone elegance.

Do not miss the lovely and peaceful abbey of La Cambre. At the far end of the chaussée d'Ixelles is the first of the chain of Ixelles Lakes. These are beautiful at all times, but a memorable sight in the spring when the great chestnuts are in bloom. Beyond the lakes, in a gentle glade, lies the abbey, and though only a part of the complex of buildings, the former convent church and cloisters, is now used for ecclesiastical purposes, I do not think that you will regret any effort you make to visit this beautiful spot.

The Abbaye de la Cambre was Cistercian and was founded in 1201 by a Brussels lady named Giselle, who obtained a grant of land from the then Duke of Brabant for the purpose. Its name derives from Onze Lieve Vrouw Camer—'House of Our Blessed Lady'. Nobles and burghers of Brussels greatly helped the nuns to establish themselves, and they remained there until the wars of religion in the sixteenth century forced them to leave the place for a time. On return they again prospered, but with the French Revolution all religious orders were suppressed and the community was dissolved, its last abbess being the Lady Seraphine Snoy. The buildings were annexed by the State and sold, part to a girls' boarding-school and part to a cotton spinner. Since 1847, however, there has been much restoration; later a division into three was achieved. The convent church, the cloisters and adjoining buildings belong to the parish of Saint Philip Neri, and the remainder is shared between the Army Geographical Institute and an art school.

The terraced gardens, open to the public, have a delightful lake, and the whole is exactly as laid out by one of the abbesses, who was Italian. The church is fourteenth- and fifteenth-century and of a moving simplicity and dignity. It contains a fine picture of 'Christ Crowned with Thorns' which is the work of the fifteenth-century Flemish painter Dirck Bouts. In the courtyard is a storeyed doorway of stone with the armorial blazon of the last abbess. Modern frescoes in the cloisters illustrating the life of Saint Alice, who was a nun of La Cambre, are worthy of note. Among other illustrious people who have lived or stayed in the abbey are Saint Boniface, and the widow of Count Egmont, who fled there from the Egmont Palace in Brussels with her eleven children after the execution of her husband in the Grand' Place.

There is on the outskirts of Brussels one place of surpassing interest and beauty, a house which still seems to shelter the spirit of the celebrated scholar who once lived in it. This is to be found in the village-suburb of Anderlecht, which is now being absorbed and will soon be embraced by the growth of the city in that direction.

On the former village green, opposite its church of Saint Guidon, is a sturdy oak door in a high wall of ancient brick. Tall trees peer over the wall, and the door opens on to a quiet paradise of a garden, filled with flower scents and the voices of birds. Here is the house of Erasmus, the gentle philosopher who in his time was the friend of half the famous intellects of the world. Whether he, as a scholar, interests the visitor or not, a walk through his home is a treat of the highest order, for here is the dwelling-place of a man of culture of four hundred years ago, with the books, the desk, cupboards, inkstand and chair that he used, still in their places in his study. Few visitors can easily tear themselves away from the door of the superb Long Room, and few can restrain a cry of delight at its beauty when they top the steps leading to it and gaze down its length. The magnificent coffered ceiling, in ancient silver-fawn oak wood, the range of beautiful mullioned and diamond-paned windows looking on to the garden, the ancient floor of adzed planks polished by time to the colour of a still pool in autumn woods, combine to form a tableau of perfection. The walls are covered in splendid hangings of Cordova leather, on which an embossed pattern in mellow gold stands out against a background of softest bluish-jade, and around them are ranged the high-backed, square-framed chairs with their tawny leather seats and gleaming brass nails, the tall Spanish and Flemish cupboards of finest oak and walnut, with their wrought-iron latches and hinges, which are marks of the place and period. The view of Erasmus's Long Room from its doorway is something you will not soon forget.

Across the village green is the now disused Béguinage of Anderlecht. The Béguines of Belgium are a religious order of women; they enter upon community life for only so long as they wish, instead of taking perpetual vows, in order to give a part of their lives to prayer and work: a year, or three, or five. In some places the Béguinages have been closed, as here, but at Ghent, Courtrai and Bruges they are still in use. Each Béguine had her own abode ('one up, one down') and a scrap of garden, and they met in a common room for work such as sewing or study, and had a common chapel. Here at Anderlecht you can see the typical Béguine home, of the most Spartan simplicity, with its contemporary furniture and appointments, and as you stand in this peaceful square when you leave, you can imagine the gentle, half-smiling Erasmus, so well known in feature from Holbein's portraits of him, seated at his writing-table on one side of the old church, while on the other the busy needles of the Béguines flew in and out of their eternal sewing for the poor.

Chapter 9

After Dark

'BRUSSELS is delightful at any time of the day,' said one of its residents, 'but after dark, ah, then it is magic.'

Belgium knows as well as any country the possibilities of floodlighting, and the Grand' Place of Brussels after nightfall becomes a wonderland. But there are many other bits of highly successful floodlighting which no visitor must miss. The Palais de Justice, almost too overpowering by day, takes on by night a less heavy look and becomes a great silver treasure chest dominating the city. Away at the other end of it the new National Basilica of the Koekelberg, which in daylight is of a style somewhat too exotic for north-west Europe, becomes at night altogether more friendly and familiar, and the still newer Atomium, though almost an intruder from the world of tomorrow, loses its rather alarming over-scientific look, and turns into a glittering, multicoloured bauble for the Christmas tree of the Giant's Child.

The towers of the Cathedral of Saint Gudule, the lions on guard at the Tomb of the Unknown Warrior, the soaring triumph-song of the Cinquantenaire Arch, the stone lace of Notre-Dame du Sablon, the sturdy bronze tradesmen who stand about Counts Egmont and Hoorn, the giggle of Manneken-Pis, the columns of the Parliament House, the rows of glittering windows of the royal palace, even the green, living curtains which surround the Parc de Bruxelles, are all sought out and transformed by the miracle-working fingers of the floodlights. And everywhere in the score or so of public gardens of the city the magic of the floodlighting of flowers, pools, lawns, trees and statuary, nearly always most effectively coloured, is exploited to the utmost.

Brussels has many times been called 'La Ville Lumière', and the wonderful array of her commercial electric signs is something to remember. In the rue Neuve and the rue du Midi, the boulevard Anspach and the boulevard Adolphe Max, and on the place de Brouckère, they turn the night into a riotous carnival of colour, movement and fun. On the place de Brouckère you can quite happily stand for half an hour watching this animated performance, for here is the commercial heart of the city.

On the least excuse, or none at all that is discoverable, whole parishes of Brussels in the middle-class quarters and the working districts burst forth into a frenzy of street decoration, with bunting, flags, pictures, cut-outs of heroic size, and even hearthrugs and tablecloths hung on the walls by day, and at night crisscrossed chains of many-coloured electric lights, from which hang stars, lions, horses' heads, colossal balloons and revolving wheels. The great puzzle to the visitor is how the quiet, steady functioning of the traffic-lights is distinguishable at all through this crazy kaleidoscope of colour and movement, but they do seem to work, for the traffic flows easily and very fast.

All this varied entertainment is free of charge, of course, to anyone who will take the trouble to stroll through the right streets, or to move from one quarter to another by bus or tram. But Brussels is a very fascinating centre of evening attractions too, for those who have a little money to spend.

For opera and ballet you go to the large and famous Théâtre Royale de la Monnaie (Royal Mint Theatre), and here, sooner or later, you will find companies of international renown from all over the world. This Royal Mint Theatre, so called from an ancient mint which once occupied its site, has a place in Belgian history, because in July 1830 patriotic feeling was so stirred up by a performance there of a play called *The Dumb Girl of Portici* that the audience rose to their feet, rushed from the theatre and

fell to fighting in the streets, and this disturbance developed into
the revolution which resulted in the nation's declaration of independence. The theatre has therefore a very special place in the
hearts of all Belgian people. At two of the other Brussels theatres,
Le Parc and Les Galeries, French companies often try out new
productions before they are put on in Paris.

The Palais des Beaux Arts has two fine concert halls, and in
this place you never know what you might hear. All through the
season the most exciting menu is put on, and the only way to find
out in advance is to watch the newspapers and street posters.
Everything depends upon just when you happen to be visiting
Brussels. For example, the last time I was there I discovered only
two nights before their concert that I could hear the world-famous
choir of men and boys from the Sistine Chapel in the Vatican at
Rome, who were touring the Continent's capitals.

The Palais des Beaux Arts also has a cinema museum, and that
does not only mean that some very remarkable early contraptions
for producing 'living pictures' are on view—which is certainly
the case—but that the place has a comprehensive library of all
that is best in films of the past, and these are regularly shown in
the theatre there. Anyone in Brussels for as much as a week is sure
to be able to see at least one film which has given real pleasure in
years gone by, and which cannot now be seen in any ordinary
cinema. But the film theatre only holds very few people, and early
inquiry and booking are needed.

Cinemas in general are excellent in Brussels, and important
new films are released there as soon as in any other capital in
Europe. It is worth remembering that on written request the
Brussels Radio Centre issues free tickets for orchestral and solo
vocal and instrumental concerts in its own broadcasting theatre.
Late entry is not allowed, but in all other respects one might be in
any first-class concert hall in any large city. One thing needs to be
borne in mind about getting there: the 16 or 17 tram from the
porte de Namur drops you quite near to the public square where

AFTER DARK 67

the theatre is to be found, but though this square is named the
place Eugène Flagey, nobody in Brussels seems to know it by
any other name than the place Sainte Croix.

Belgium, and of course Brussels, dearly loves a circus. During
the summer season there is usually one ready to perform, its
'Big Top' set up for two weeks or three on some cleared bomb-
site or in one or other of the public squares in the working-class
districts. The best of these is named Knie, and red-and-white
sticker-slips appear everywhere, on walls, lamp-posts and the
'pepper-pot' advertisement kiosks on pavement corners: 'Cirque
Knie, Place So-and-So', with the dates and times of performances.
Seats are bookable at the spot, and are not expensive. Cirque
Knie is too good to be missed; its clowns are first class, and—it
can only be seen on the Continent. You pronounce it 'K-nie' when
inquiring your way.

Everyone in Brussels will tell you: 'You haven't seen Brussels
by night if you haven't seen the night club "Bœuf sur le Toît".'
Certainly it is elaborately decorated; certainly it is not nearly big
enough for the crowd who seek it out—it is near the Cinquantenaire Arch; certainly the lighting is so dim that you need half
an hour to become accustomed to the gloom; certainly there is a
good orchestra. Certainly also there is a succession of strip-tease
and other acts up to 5 a.m., and you can always depend upon
seeing some brilliant acrobats and jugglers. But equally certainly
the glass dance-floor is scarcely bigger than a bath-mat, and the
drinks provided are scandalously expensive. In all these respects
it is like a score of other night clubs, in Brussels and elsewhere,
and most people will gain more interest and pleasure from an
evening stroll along the boulevards to the porte de Namur, where
in a short time the visitor can see the world and his wife (or his
teenage girl friend) strolling also along the gay lines of lighted
shop windows, wandering in and out of the numerous cafés arm
in arm and chatting in half the languages of Europe.

Music-halls have almost died out where they formerly

flourished, but Brussels has a wonderful one: Ancienne Belgique, in the rue des Pierres. Ancienne Belgique is known the world over; it is not so much a place of entertainment as a national institution, and its second affectionately given name of 'The Grown-ups' Kindergarten' gives an idea of the robust and simple pleasures which it offers to ordinary people evening after evening. The walls of the vast hall are covered with mural paintings of the beauties of Belgian cities, so that the Citadel of Namur peers over the shoulder of the belfry of Bruges; the Steen fortress at Antwerp stands cheek by jowl with the Château des Comtes at Ghent, and all are well mixed up with a jumble of canals, gables, turrets and narrow gateways. On the floor are set square lino-topped tables, affording seating for (believe it or not) two thousand patrons, and here you must drink if you are to see the show. But you can ask for an *eau minérale*—and you can spin it out for a surprisingly long time.

The two great things to be seen are the audience and the show, and in that order of importance. You will see a perfect example of a 'populaire' crowd, and you can make up a fresh story for every group at every table within your range of vision. And how whole-heartedly they enjoy themselves. The very sound of their gales of laughter is a tonic. A part of the show on the huge stage—'pop' singing, old-fashioned ballad singers, tellers of comic stories and patter—will be lost on the foreigner, for speech is rapid, jokes are topical and much 'Bruxellois' is used, but there will also be a superb collection of 'turns'—acrobats, jugglers, contortionists, trapeze and high-wire artists, conjurors, brilliant purveyors of mime. There is also more than likely to be some glorious fooling with à trombone, or a bicycle, or a washing-machine, which may or may not fall to pieces. My own out-standing memory from there is of two clowns who most heart-rendingly 'ruined' each other's attempts to play a violin duet with many appalling squeaks, wails and false starts. Their act ended when one leapt suddenly upon the shoulders of the other and sat there, leaning sideways and bowing the instrument tucked beneath his own chin, while his partner reached up to hold and finger it. At the same time, by a long stretch of his left arm, he reached down to finger the other violin, held under his companion's chin and bowed by him. The pair gave a very good two-part rendering of 'Waltzing Matilda', while the one man with his feet on the ground raced round and round the stage in frenzied circles, carrying his lighter partner on his back. It was at the close of the applause given to that act that a hand-sized patch of plaster fell from the ceiling of the hall—and no one seemed in the least surprised.

Yes, Ancienne Belgique is a 'must'. It is entertainment for the masses, but you will remember, as long as the turns on the stage, the colourful scrapbook of humanity all round you, enjoying themselves to the top of their bent as Mr and Mrs Ordinary Belgian so well know how. And it is a programme to which any visitor can take his children, which is more than can be said for some of the top-class night clubs not many hundred yards away. Not for nothing is Ancienne Belgique called by yet a third name: 'The Trampoline of Good Humour.'

Chapter 10

Brussels Boasts

AND so she should. Some say that she does not boast half enough. But she has much to boast of; much that is unique, but that she seems to take very much for granted and to make the subject of no display. In this chapter she is to be taken firmly by the shoulders and made to boast, so that some of these things may be known.

Brussels had the first railway on the Continent. It was King Leopold I who most promptly and clearly realized the crossroads position which his capital held in north-western Europe. It should, he felt, be fitted to retain and strengthen that position in the age of mechanical transport by all possible means. So in 1835 he proposed the construction of, and finally inaugurated, the first railway on the continent of Europe, to run from the gates of Brussels to the city of Malines.

That railway line started from a spot known as the Allée Verte—the Green Avenue. The name still exists, and now, instead of being the starting-point of a railway line, it is the 'town' port of call for a helicopter service, for Belgium was again among the most far-seeing countries in Europe when she recognized the value of the helicopter for use on regular routes between town centre and town centre. There are now services twice daily from Brussels to Rotterdam, and once daily to Cologne, calling at several places on the way over both routes. Passengers in transit by international airline are picked up by helicopter at the main Brussels airport of Melsbroeck.

What else had Brussels first in Europe? Well—the first gasworks and the first shopping arcade. The Galeries Saint-Hubert, and there are indeed two: the Galerie du Roi and the Galerie de la Reine, are old and fine and dignified, and there are first-class, if not very large, shops for the sale of such things as antiques, jewellery, perfumes and cosmetics, the most exclusive of men's ties and the most exquisite of ladies' blouses. At the time when they were opened, shopping under cover was unheard of in Europe.

Brussels really is proud of two things, and with good reason. One of these is to be found in another very beautiful shopping arcade—the Galerie Ravenstein, so named because it stands opposite the Hôtel Ravenstein, a former residence of the Burgundian dukes and the only architectural relic of them left in Brussels. It is the Brussels Record Library, a branch of the National Record Library which is under the patronage of the Queen Dowager of Belgium, the brilliant and beloved 'Reine Elisabeth', who has done so much for music in her country. The Brussels Discothèque is a surprisingly unimportant looking place; you might be forgiven for thinking that you were in 'just another record shop', but the few records on display are only a sample of the riches stored away behind the scenes.

There are records in a round dozen of branches—classical and folk music, 'pop' songs, children's music, rhymes and stories, literary masterpieces read by famous voices, documentary recordings of important ceremonies and of great moments in history, language records of all kinds, readings from Scripture and choral renderings of liturgical music, the *manifestations folkloriques* of Belgium, plays grave and gay, jazz, Greek tragedy and drama in the original, all made accessible within moments by the remarkably efficient cataloguing and filing system. For a very reasonable charge families, clubs, schools, individuals and music and language-study groups have the run of this vast store of material; records may be borrowed by the week to take away and are renewable exactly as are library books.

Queen Elisabeth, widow of King Albert I, who is herself a violinist of the front rank, has instituted at the royal estate of Argenteuil near Brussels a 'chapelle musicale' for concerts of chamber music, and also an annual international music contest for young pianists, violinists and composers which bears her name. Some hundreds of entrants, the cream of the younger musical life in their respective countries, take part before a distinguished panel of adjudicators, the awards carrying extremely high prestige. The competitions are held in the Brussels Musée des Beaux Arts, and each year attract more and more entrants.

The city's other great source of pride is its ultra-modern, ultra-efficient central sorting office for postal material, the first in Europe to be electronically operated. It had to be built on an exceptionally awkward site beside the Midi station in order to be near enough to the southern terminus. The plot available was only about 350 feet long and less than 50 feet wide. The difficulty was overcome by building upwards and employing vertical mechanization, by means of which the mailbags, after entering at street (ground floor) level or railway (first floor) level, pass up a northward ascending trunk, are dealt with on several floors, and then come back to rail or street level through a southward descending trunk. In the building are six glassed-in control cabins, from each of which an official can direct the work of an entire floor by means of the switch panel before him. The centre is able to handle a total of fifteen million pieces of mail of all kinds —letters, postcards, parcels and circulars—each week. This great modern office holds a leading position in the chain of European postal services.

From all quarters of the city can be seen the vast International Centre expressly aimed at being of use to the thousands of people from all parts of the world who come to Brussels for the varied assortment of conferences which now take place there. This is housed in a building which is known as the Rogier International Centre, and has been built on the whole area formerly occupied by the Brussels Nord station. The large open space in front of this station was called place Rogier, which accounts for the new centre's name.

Rogier Centre took four years to build and covers almost ten thousand square yards. Its main portion, which has a fine curved frontage, runs to nine floors, but there is a tower at one end, entirely faced with glass, fronting the place Rogier, of which part is twenty-six and part thirty floors high. At 117 metres from the ground the top of this tower is almost exactly fifty feet higher than the Atomium.

Here are a few of the facilities which the centre provides for business visitors to Brussels. There are 85 shops, running to three floors each; 155 very large residential flats for short-term hire; 600 offices which can similarly be rented, and a round-the-clock service of multilingual shorthand typists. In addition, printing, duplicating, translation and interpreting are all available. There is a good exhibition hall, a medical centre, a service station for cars (not to mention parking space for 1,000 of them on five floors), an urban and a country bus station, a bank, post office, currency exchange and several restaurants. In the tower is the fastest lift in Europe, capable of taking fifteen persons at nearly twenty feet a second direct to the Martini Room on the top floor, where receptions and parties can be held. It may be added that this enormous building has 3,200 internal doors and over 10,000 electric light points.

Centre Rogier stands on a part of the Inner Ring Road which is named boulevard d'Anvers, and a short way from it this changes its name to boulevard du Jardin Botanique. The Botanical Gardens here, which give their name to the fine wide avenue, are not new, but Brussels is rightly proud of them, and especially of the enormous Palm House.

Across the boulevard from the Palm House is a remarkable school, the Institut Saint-Louis, which combines, in one vast educational complex, primary, high school and further education,

F

leading to university level. It grants its own diplomas in the
arts and sciences and also in commerce, and being a 'religious'
foundation it passes the majority of its students on to the Catholic
University of Louvain.

The city is also distinguished for a study-group of famous
scholars known as the Bollandists. These eminent men take their
name from their founder, Father Bolland, who in the early
seventeenth century began an intensive study of the lives of the
saints. This work still goes on, and the group publishes from
time to time new facts they have discovered, either in book form
or in articles written for their own magazine. Manuscripts of
their earliest researches form part of the treasure in the Royal
Library.

Brussels has one unique museum which in the ordinary sense
is not a museum at all. It is really a gigantic collection of superbly
finished photographs. These are housed by themselves in a
specially constructed building near the Cinquantenaire Arch, and
the collection is called the Patrimoine Nationale, which might be
translated as 'Our National Heritage'. It constitutes a photo-
graphic record, constantly being added to, of everything old in
the country that is man-made and interesting; those are the only
two qualifications. There are photographs of whole buildings, of
parts of them such as doorways, staircases and windows, and of
details from their decoration. Other pieces of man-made work,
such as carvings, panelling and so on, are included.

As in the case of the Record Library, its remarkable filing
system and cross-referenced index are of great importance.
Suppose that an old house, for example in Liège, in south-eastern
Belgium, had a fine staircase with a wrought-iron handrail
showing angels' heads. You would be able to trace this under
just whatever scrap of fact you happened to remember about it:
staircases, wrought-iron work, handrails, private houses, city of
Liège, angels. Every one of these separate references would bring
you in the end to the same numbered portfolio of photographs,

in the numbered fireproof shelves, and in a matter of minutes the photograph you wanted could be found and laid out for your inspection, possibly with other wrought-iron staircase rails from other parts of the country, for comparison.

Melsbroeck airport a few years ago looked more like a country sports ground with a rather pretty pavilion on it than an international airport. Its construction was begun by the Germans during the second world war, but since then it has been vastly enlarged and is now most efficient and up to date. Its confines have spread so that it now seems almost to have thrown its arms round the ancient Château of Steenockerzeel, and its buildings include a Catholic chapel and an hotel for passengers in transit. Between 1949 and 1963 the total number of passengers handled rose from 74,000 to 800,000, while annual freightage records rose from 1,270 to 20,000 tons, and at this figure it represents 8 per cent of all Belgium's commercial exchange dealings.

Sabena (Société Anonyme Belge de Navigation Aéronautique), the national air-line, is the owner of the fine air terminal, providing every imaginable amenity for the arriving, departing or transit traveller. Anyone leaving the new and very modern Gare Centrale at Brussels has only to cross the street from the station's main entrance to be received into its welcoming arms. Brussels set itself determinedly to cut out the loss at ground level of the time gained by air travel, and as a result the National Airport is now one of the most easily accessible of all the world's main skyways. A rail-car service runs the fourteen kilometres between the airport and the Sabena Terminal in central Brussels in sixteen minutes.

The great National Theatre of Belgium, one of the amenities housed in the Rogier Centre, is something to marvel at in its sheer size, its up-to-dateness and its efficiency, and anyone gaining entry for a complete tour of this place, bewildering as it is, should be prepared to give up not less than half a day to seeing all its phases.

The idea of a National Theatre which would be much more than a large seating-place where plays would be performed was first mooted in 1945. It was to be a living organism with a four-fold aim:

to produce front-rank plays and to assure the widest possible diffusion of their performances over the country;

to improve the skill, the lot and the status of the Belgian actor;

to witness to the cultural life of Belgium in places overseas;

to be at once a fixed and permanent home for all that is meant by 'theatre' within Brussels itself, and a force of performers bringing all the pleasures of playgoing to towns and villages in Belgium and to the chief cities of foreign countries.

Within fifteen years it had put on 8,000 performances of 169 different works, ranging from Sophocles to Arthur Miller and from Dürrenmatt to Shakespeare, with preference for classical French works and those of Belgian playrights.

The auditorium has 765 seats, every one facing the stage, and none more than 75 feet from it. Its designer formulated two principles, which he said his theatre must follow: when the house lights are on it must appear brilliant and glowing, so as to produce a feeling of well-being in the audience, yet at the same time to give to evening dresses and any uniforms which might be worn their full colour value. When they are lowered all brilliance must disappear, giving place to 'une boîte tout à fait obscure, afin de concentrer au maximum l'attention du public vers la scène'.

Accordingly the walls are lined with closely gathered non-inflammable black tulle, behind which are disposed numerous light projectors, and in the ceiling are 1,200 spotlights. As the steel curtain rises all these light-sources begin progressively to dim, and the tulle walls become 'aussi opaque qu'un rideau de velours noir'.

There is another auditorium seating only about three hundred, called the 'Theatrical Workshop', which can be very quickly

adapted to Greek, Italian or Elizabethan settings, and even to
'Theatre in the Round'. Here much dramatic experimentation is
carried on.

Mechanization is advanced to its fullest limits, in scene-
changing, in lighting, in air-conditioning. Even the technicians
working out of sight, high above the stage, mount to their lofty
perch by an express lift. The chief electrician can make, electronically in advance, punched-card records of the lighting
changes required, so that there is no possibility of error once the
console has been switched on. Music can be produced on the
great organ in the same way.

The theatre has a complex of fascinating workshops behind
the scenes: factories, as it were, for producing furniture and
such accessories as sedan chairs and hand-carts; dressmaking,
tailoring and shoemaking rooms; wigmakers' shops; fitting-
rooms and scene-painting studios. Whole corridors are occupied
by dressing-rooms for players, and there are also a lounge for
them, a rehearsal theatre and an extremely comprehensive library
of works of help and interest to theatrical people. It is not surprising that this theatre itself claims to 'participate with all
its forces in the contemporary worldwide movement for the re-
surgence of a truly popular theatre'.

Brussels has also an electronic music studio. The use of
electricity to produce musical sound waves has been an interest
of man for many years, ever since, in fact, the invention of the
telephone by Alexander Graham Bell. Some of the big electrical
concerns, as for example Philips of Holland and Siemens of
Germany, maintain their own research studios in this branch,
and others are subsidized by governments, universities and
broadcasting corporations. But there are only two private electronic music studios, and one of them is in Brussels. This was
founded in 1958 by three friends: a violinist, an electronics engineer and a composer. The works which have left the studio since,
notably a version of *Electra* and the sound track for a film about

Liège, have given Belgium a well-earned place in the world of electronic music.

I.N.R. (Institut National de Radiodiffusion) holds as big a place in Belgian life and affairs as the broadcasting corporations of any country do in their own home: concerts, plays, lectures, comedy and musical shows, with documentary programmes, folklore festivals and full bulletins of news going out in both languages of the country, French and Flemish. Its parent society, a piece of private enterprise, was called 'Radio-Belgique', and it started in a way so modest as to seem almost amusing by to-day's standards. Its transmitter was of $1\frac{1}{2}$ kilowatts only, very little more than that of a single-bar electric heater! There was 'one engineer, and one technician. . . . Later, the engineer having been done away with'—the account does not say how—'there remained only the technician'.

The traffic police of Brussels, one must imagine, live solely on a diet of headache powders. For the parking problem here is as serious as anywhere in the world, even though Brussels is by no means a large city. The old town was a maze of narrow streets, and its authorities have had a heavy backlog of widening and modernization to do. A great impetus was given to this work by the demands of the 1958 exhibition, when so heavy an influx of visitors was inevitable for the whole of the summer. Plans were made in good time: a new motorway was cut from the coast to Brussels, and within the capital itself a north-to-south arterial avenue, with numerous traffic tunnels and fly-overs to avoid junction roads from east to west which would otherwise have had to cross it.

Traffic police are quite distinct from the judiciary force, and it is worth pausing a moment to watch a man on point duty at, say, the place de Brouckère, where, often mounted on a white-painted wooden 'pulpit', he will imperturbably direct a stream of traffic flowing around him in, and from, all directions, his white *perce-neige*, the helmet which is a part of the uniform—the rest of the force wears the *képi*—shining out of the turmoil like the top of a lighthouse in a rough sea.

The chief constable of Brussels told me that thirty to thirty-five thousand vehicles seek parking-space in the city each day, and that there is now beginning a twenty-five year plan which will eventually provide a hundred thousand places and completely remake the city centre. (Needless to say, the lovely Grand' Place will never be altered.) Two great tunnels in the avenue Louise already give space for fifteen to sixteen thousand parkings.

As you go about Brussels you will most certainly notice many a place where the city has registered its pride in some illustrious personage who at some time or other has lived there, by placing a plaque on the wall of the house he occupied. One of these was a little boy who stayed in a Brussels hotel with his parents. It was in 1763 that the young Mozart, when at the height of his fame as a child prodigy, arrived there in the course of a European tour. He gave a recital at the Palace of Nassau, now the Museum of Modern Art, and it was a very brilliant occasion. While in Brussels, where the family stayed three months, the child, then just over seven years of age, composed the *allegro* movement of his Sonata No. 1 in C.

Among other exiles from France, often so politically disturbed, Victor Hugo, the author of *Les Misérables*, *The Toilers of the Sea*, *The Hunchback of Notre Dame* and many other novels, lived with his family for a time at the house on the Grand' Place known as Le Pigeon. Here he was often visited by Burgomaster de Brouckère, who laid out so much of the Brussels of today. The novelist wrote very charmingly of the Burgomaster's kindness to him and to other exiles.

At the same time as Hugo in Brussels, another man of letters from France, Alexandre Dumas, took refuge there for the same reason. He found a large house on the boulevard de Waterloo, and while there wrote *The Queen's Necklace*, a story of Marie Antoinette. Political refugees sheltering in Brussels at this time seem to have made a café near the cathedral, called In 't Voṣke (The Fox Cub), their meeting-place, and its name is still preserved.

On the roof of the Royal Mews is an attractive sculpture of a very absorbed cherub, half sprawling over a terrestrial globe, which his fat hands are trying to measure with a pair of geometrical dividers. It is called 'L'Amour Géographe', and is the work of Rodin, whose impressive seated figure, 'The Thinker', is the most familiar of his masterpieces. Young, still unknown, and a struggling 'ornament-maker', Rodin endured six hard years in Brussels before he was commissioned to produce the great sculptures on the façade of the city's Bourse.

No. 64 rue Royale bears a plaque stating that here lived the Duke of Wellington. The general was in the city several times, but his most important stay began three weeks after the escape of Napoleon from Elba and lasted until the battle of Waterloo. He was called urgently away, the night before, from the cele- brated 'Duchess of Richmond's Ball', which she was giving in her rented mansion in the rue de la Blanchisserie.

Lord Byron lived for a time at rue Ducale 51, and while there wrote a canto of *Childe Harold's Pilgrimage*. The Corsican lieutenant who later became Emperor of France stayed on two occasions in Brussels, each time with a different wife. With Josephine de Beauharnais he stayed nine days at the Palace of Laeken, and later he brought the Impératrice Marie-Louise there. To him the Palace owes the fact that it still exists. It had served as official residence of the governors of the Netherlands during the Austrian period, but stood empty for many years after 1794. It was on the eve of demolition when Napoleon acquired it privately and renovated it. Two visits, however, of nine days and of three weeks were all the use he ever made of it in person.

Charlotte and Emily Brontë arrived in the city in 1842, to become pupils in a 'school for young ladies'. Before long the head of the school realized that there was little more that he could teach them, and he offered them the opportunity to become teachers themselves, Charlotte of English and Emily of music. Unknown to her employer, Constantin Héger, Charlotte fell in love with him, but the romance was brought to an end when the girls were recalled to England by the illness of their father. Two of Charlotte's novels, however, strongly reflect this period: *Jane Eyre*, which is considered to be largely autobiographical, and *Villette*, where the city described is Brussels, and where Professor Héger appears as Monsieur Paul.

Three-quarters of a century later another Englishwoman worked in Brussels, the devoted nurse Edith Cavell. Famous Belgians who have been residents include de Brouckère, André Vésale, the sixteenth-century anatomist, and the redoubtable Burgomaster Adolphe Max, of the early days of the first world war.

In other places in this book Brussels has been thought of as Europe's conference centre. Many trade and scientific exhibitions and conferences are staged at the Rogier Centre, but the larger ones must use the hall known as the Centenaire, which was erected at Heysel, to house part of the World Fair of 1958. But the city has also the great Palais des Congrès, part of the complex of buildings known as the Mont des Arts. Near here is the seat of the European Common Market, and that of Benelux, the customs union of Belgium, the Netherlands and Luxembourg, which does so much for the trade of the three member-countries.

The existence of these conference centres in Brussels points to and highlights the city's awareness of the social duty laid upon it by its geographical position, to welcome all who come, and by so doing promote the welfare of modern Europe and of the wider world outside—a function which may, and should, be one of its proudest boasts.

Chapter 11

Too Much is not Enough

BRUSSELS must be felt as well as seen. Fine old buildings, a wealth of art treasures, colourful gardens and outdoor markets, good music, gay streets day and night, and architecture which looks back out of tomorrow on to today—all these are to be found, together with other delights. But there is much more: an essence, almost a living spirit, created in and for this city by her geography and by her history. Most of all, perhaps, by her people.

Once there was a river in Brussels—a narrow and unimportant stream, named the Senne, which during the last century disappeared from sight under the vaultings ordered by Leopold II. Narrow, shallow, and now concealed for ever, it yet makes its strong mark upon Brussels, for along the line of its course there runs that visible difference in level, and that other intangible and indefinable difference which cleaves the city in two, even today. On the right bank, elegance, culture, cosmopolitan grace. On the left, the ceaseless clatter of trade and commerce, overflowing bonhomie, rubust enjoyment, the earthy exuberance of the peasant. Yet the two are one—though they rarely meet as friends —for both are Bruxellois.

Half of Europe has swept through Brussels, leaving traces everywhere, in language, art, music, architecture, even in personal names and family names. Despite his conquest of Gaul, the Roman left few traces, beyond these last, but Marius and César may still sit side by side in a kindergarten, and the shop of Mme Fabritius may face that of M. Ambiorix across a street.

In noble houses of upper Brussels may be seen the interior

elegance and grace of old Vienna; in the city's commercial quarter the nineteenth-century solidity of contemporary Paris; in the old town, scraps of Burgundian fortification, of Spanish fancy, of Dutch design in gable and courtyard and whitewashed cottage.

For Brussels, despite the demands of present-day housing, which have compelled the building of vast apartment blocks, is essentially a city of the individual house, the family-owned cottage.

Is there a common denominator to be found in all these assorted stocks which have gone to the making of the people of Brussels? Indeed, yes; a label can be attached to one and all of them, bearing the single word 'Energy', for this is the hallmark of the Bruxellois, of his wife and of his children. Energy for work of hand and brain, for sport, for fun and laughter, even for eating! In short, energy for the enjoyment of life to the full. There lies the character of the Belgian capital, as built in its people.

The Bruxellois is a thorough-going extrovert, interested in everything that goes on around him. The least incident on a pavement: the upsetting of a crate of tomatoes, the blowing away of a score of leaflets let fall by a distributor, will collect its handful of eager onlookers in a few seconds. In the train or tram going to work there is no trace of dourness; any grumbles will be half-laughing ones; conversation will be animated and general. If the occupants of all the neighbouring seats are strangers—well, qu'importe, ça? There is always le cycling, le football, the next (or the last) street procession to discuss. Why bury oneself behind a newspaper? Newspapers are many, and they are packed with news, but they can be read at home this evening, when there are no fascinating strangers to talk to. How much quicker and simpler to pick up, in the course of a chat at the café or on the bus, most of what the headlines could tell.

The Bruxellois has many loves in life: his religion; a neat home (he will repaint its exterior every year or so), a garden if possible or, if not, some tubs in a yard, with an array of staggeringly gigantic dahlias; a brass band to listen to; a procession or a game of pelota to watch; a cycle- or pigeon-race to work up his excitement; a glass of beer, and of course, enough *frites*. In all these things 'enough' is a term impossible to evaluate; his capacity for them is unlimited.

Within the Bruxellois, side by side with his energy, is an unexpected placidity; when his city is half-gutted by war he sets to and rebuilds it, in the style of the moment or in that of a few years hence, and then gets on with his enjoyment of life where he left off.

The Bruxellois, despite the size of the place he lives in, is still to a great extent a countryman turned town-dweller; he was after all a *paysan*, in the truest sense of that word, when he began to populate the city. There is still a strong and very natural feeling of 'commune' and of 'parish'; the type of lamp-post will change abruptly as you go along a street, and your feet step from cobbling to asphalt between a shop and its neighbour. The *képi* of the *agent de police* at one corner will be of a different design from that of the man on the next. The streets bordering two sides of a block will be *en kermesse*, which is to say celebrating a carnival, while those on the other two are carrying on with workaday routine. There is too, in all the *populaire* quarters, a real pleasure in that ingrained countryman's habit of bringing a chair out on to the pavement to enjoy a smoke and the paper or a chat, when the day's work is done. He has, in short, preserved something very precious of the village mentality.

Above all, this city is friendly. It stands at the cross-roads of western Europe, but that fact would not of itself create such a quality. Though the very stones of Brussels have their voice, this friendliness must show itself first, last and all the time through its people. And it does just that. It is not only on the street-map that Brussels is a *cité en forme de cœur*.

Index

85